Catherine Atkinson has a degree in Fo[...] restaurants including the Roux Broth[...] Cookery Editor on *Woman's Weekly* and [...] now a full-time writer and food consu[...] and has written more than fifty cookbooks, including, *Cookies, Biscuits, Bars and Brownies* (winner in the best dessert category of the Gourmand World Awards). She is also the author of *Brilliant Breadmaking in your Bread Machine* and *How To Make Perfect Panini*.

Also available from Robinson

Afternoon Tea
Everyday Bread from Your Bread Machine
Everyday Curries
Everyday Lebanese Cooking
Everyday Thai Cooking
How To Make Perfect Panini
Soups for Every Season
Southern Italian Family Cooking
Traditional Country Preserving

How to Make Your Own Cordials and Syrups

Catherine Atkinson

ROBINSON

ROBINSON

First published in Great Britain in 2015 by Robinson

Typeset in Great Britain by Basement Press, Glaisdale
Printed and bound in Great Britain by Clays Ltd, Elcograf S.p.A.

Papers used by Robinson are from well-managed forests
and other responsible sources

Robinson
An imprint of
Little, Brown Book Group
Carmelite House
50 Victoria Embankment
London EC4Y 0DZ

An Hachette UK Company
www.hachette.co.uk

www.littlebrown.co.uk

How To Books are published by Robinson, a part of Little, Brown Book Group.
We welcome proposals from authors who have first-hand experience of their
subjects. Please set out the aims of your book, its target market and its
suggested contents in an email to howtobooks@littlebrown.co.uk

Contents

Introduction

There's nothing quite like a refreshing glass of iced cordial on a hot summer's day, or sipping a warming indulgent liqueur in the middle of winter. How much more pleasurable it is when you have made these drinks yourself. Gardens, lanes and woods have an abundance of edible flowers, berries and plants that can easily be turned into delicious cordials, syrups and infused alcoholic tipples. And, while most fruit can be bought out of season, there is no comparison to that which is grown and picked at the time nature intended, whether you grow your own produce, buy from a local grocer or farmers' market or forage for free.

The benefits of home-made drinks are obvious. Not only do you get freshness and flavours second to none, you know exactly what's in them – no nasty additives or preservatives – and can create a drink to suit your own personal preferences. With many different drink recipes to choose from, there are plenty here that you won't find ready-made on supermarket shelves as well as those which can easily be bought but can be made at a fraction of the cost. Whether you are searching for child-friendly vitamin-packed cordials, an after-dinner liqueur or a generous and thoughtful home-made gift for friends or family, you'll find something to suit in the following chapters.

This book will take you through the basic techniques and demystify all that is essential when making cordials, syrups and other drinks – from simple, straightforward ones which can be enjoyed on the day of making, to those that take time to mature but will taste superior to the shop-bought equivalent.

The author would like to thank Lakeland Ltd who supplied bottles for testing and who sell a range of drink-making equipment at www.lakelandlimited.com.

Conversion Charts

This book provides metric measurements for the ingredients, but those who still prefer Imperial can use these conversions.

Weight

Metric	Imperial
15g	½oz
25g	1oz
50g	2oz
75g	3oz
100g	4oz
150g	5oz
175g	6oz
200g	7oz
225g	8oz
250g	9oz
300g	10oz
325g	11oz
350g	12oz
375g	13oz
400g	14oz
425g	15oz
450g	1lb
550g	1¼lb
675g	1½lb
800g	1¾lb
900g	2lb
1kg	2¼lb

Liquid

5ml	1 tsp
10ml	2 tsp
15ml	1 tbsp
50ml	2fl oz
120ml	4fl oz
150ml	¼ pint
200ml	7fl oz
250ml	8fl oz
300ml	½ pint
350ml	12fl oz
400ml	14fl oz
450ml	¾ pint
600ml	1 pint
750ml	1¼ pints
900ml	1½ pints
1 litre	1¾ pints
1.5 litres	2½ pints
1.75 litres	3 pints

Measurements

2.5cm	1 inch
5cm	2 inches
10cm	4 inches
15cm	6 inches
20cm	8 inches
25cm	10 inches
30cm	12 inches

Cordials, Syrups and Liqueurs

Essentially, cordials and syrups are made from strained fruit juice sweetened with sugar or honey. Some flowers and herbs can be used as flavourings in much the same way. The two names are interchangeable, although syrups tend to be slightly thicker. Both are diluted to taste – usually one part cordial or syrup to four or five parts water – and served as a soft drink, although they also have lots of other culinary uses.

Liqueurs are spirit-based drinks to which flavouring elements have been added, usually by infusion. Sugar is often, but not always, added to the mix to enhance the flavour, preserve it for longer and sometimes to thicken the texture. It may be added when steeping or afterwards in the form of a sugar syrup.

A Brief History

Cordials and syrups were created as a way of preserving seasonal fruits and other ingredients to enjoy during the winter months when little fresh fruit was available. They were first made in the sixteenth century when sugar was introduced to Europe from the West Indies and became a sought-after ingredient. The demand for sugar cane became so great that it encouraged the rise of colonialism and the slave trade and many drinks and cocktails such as Planter's Punch (page 147) originate from this time. In the eighteenth century, sugar beet began to be cultivated specifically for its sugar content in the western world and sugar became plentiful and relatively cheap. During the nineteenth century, making cordials and liqueurs was considered an important skill for young housewives and most of the recipes we use today are based on those created during that era. Bringing out a bottle of home-made cordial or liqueur was considered the ultimate gesture of good hospitality and in Edwardian and Victorian times would have usually been prepared by the 'lady of the house' and served to guests at any time during the day, regardless of whether it was alcoholic or not.

In the twentieth century, home-made bottled drinks became less fashionable. Many homes had less storage space and by the middle of the century refrigerators could be found in most homes, followed by freezers in the sixties and seventies. Imported produce meant that many fruits were available all year round; soft fruits could be bought in the winter months and citrus fruits never disappeared from grocers' shelves. As the range of commercially produced products increased – especially imported fruit juices, fruit-flavoured squashes and ready-made alcoholic drinks and liqueurs – the knowledge and desire to make bottled drinks diminished.

In recent years, the art of preserving has made a massive comeback. Many people prefer to make their own instead of buying mass-produced products with artificial flavourings and colourings. The satisfaction that comes from making your own drinks is being rediscovered.

Ingredients

Fruit, flowers and herbs
Many of the recipes in this book are based on ingredients that you can grow yourself, buy cheaply from the local farmers' market or even better, gather

from lanes and hedgerows for free: elderflowers, blackberries, sloes, rosehips and nettles are just a few examples. Making drinks, cordials and syrups from these will cost you little more than the price of a bag of sugar.

When foraging, choose a sunny day, as wild crops (especially flowers) tend to have a better flavour and aroma on a bright sunlit day. Avoid picking close to heavy traffic and along the edges of fields of crops which have been recently sprayed, as well as low-growing produce on dog-walking routes! Dress in sensible shoes or boots, long-sleeved T-shirts and trousers. A pair of gloves for picking among thorny bushes may be useful. You'll need plenty of plastic containers, bags and possibly a cool bag to carry your produce home. Finally, use a little common sense. Avoid trespassing and Sites of Special, Scientific Interest (SSSIs), as it is illegal to pick any plant, including the humble blackberry, in these areas. Try to pick a little from several different places, rather than stripping one area completely bare.

Preserving Ingredients

While many cordials, syrups and liqueurs can be enjoyed on the day they are made, most contain ingredients that will extend their shelf life, usually sugar and/or alcohol. There are also a few cordials and syrups which have the addition of either vinegar or citric acid, a natural preservative.

Sugar

This is not only a sweetener: it is the key preservative in cordials and syrups. It also acts as a thickener. The recipes in this book mainly use white sugar, which produces a better colour and flavour, but sometimes soft light brown sugar, demerara sugar or honey may be used in cordials, syrups and liqueurs to give a richer flavour or a more golden colour. Granulated sugar is the cheapest option and can be used in most recipes where the liquid is heated. Caster sugar may be used instead and will dissolve more quickly as the grains are much finer.

Citrus fruit and citric acid

Some cordials and syrups need an additional tang to balance the taste and to bring out the flavour. Often lemon juice is used – freshly squeezed is best – or the zest of a lemon, in which case choose unwaxed lemons, preferably organic. Citric acid is an excellent and inexpensive alternative to lemon juice and is used where you don't want to add pectin, which might make the cordial set to a jelly. It is sold as fine white crystals. It is a completely natural preservative, so will also lengthen the shelf life of your drink. If you want to substitute one for the other, one tablespoon of lemon juice is the equivalent of quarter of a teaspoon of citric acid.

Vinegar

Vinegar features in a number of old-fashioned non-alcoholic cordials as it acts as a preservative, vital in the days before refrigeration. Cordials known as 'shrubs' are a typical example and have a sweet and sour tangy taste in which extra sugar balances the vinegar. The word vinegar comes from the French *vin aigre*, meaning 'sour wine', and it is made by turning the alcohol in wine, cider or sherry into acetic acid; it's this acid that helps these cordials to keep because it prevents moulds developing. Several varieties of vinegar are typically used in cordials:

Wine vinegar may be red or white depending on the colour of the original wine. White wine vinegar is slightly milder and good for pale cordials; red wine vinegar will add colour as well, so is often used in red berry cordials such as Strawberry Shrub (page 86).

Cider vinegar has a fairly sharp taste and a fruity flavour. A small amount works well in apple and pear cordials.

Raspberry vinegar is much more expensive than wine vinegar and has a lovely fruit flavour and attractive colour. When only a small amount of vinegar is required, it is good in raspberry or mixed-berry cordials.

Yeast

This is used in some fizzy soft drinks such as ginger beer. Use fast-action (easy-blend) 'baker's' yeast rather than 'brewer's' yeast for soft drink-making. These tiny granules of yeast don't need activating before using and are readily available in supermarkets. They come in small vacuum packets or boxes of individual sachets, each containing about 7 grams or 2½ teaspoons. Always check the 'sell by' date when using yeast, as it doesn't keep long.

Base spirits

Buy good-quality base spirits for liqueurs and infusions. You don't need to use expensive premium spirits; most supermarket 'value' versions are fine, but avoid very cheap brands that you do not recognize and which may completely spoil the flavour of your liqueur.

Vodka is the perfect base for many liqueurs as it is clear and colourless and has little taste or smell, allowing the flavouring ingredients to shine. Nowadays, it is made almost exclusively from grains, mainly rye, and filtered through a layer of charcoal to remove any remaining traces of flavour. It is then bottled at an average of 37.5 per cent alcohol by volume; do not use vodkas with a lower strength than this or your liqueur will not keep as well. Many flavoured vodkas are available, but unless stated otherwise, liqueurs should always be made with an unflavoured version. Most liqueurs made with a vodka base should be served in the same way as vodka: well chilled.

Gin has a distinctive blend of herbs and aromatics, the most dominant one being juniper. There are two types: 'London dry gin' is the best known, although it doesn't actually have to be distilled in the capital. Producers of this include Gordon's, Beefeater, Belgravia and Booth's. The second type is 'Plymouth gin', which is drier with a more subtle flavour. Gin is used in many liqueurs, notably Sloe Gin (page 114)

Rum is made from sugar cane and comes in two main types: dark (or golden), which may be a clear light or very dark brown colour, including Lamb's, Captain Morgan and Old Navy, and white rum (Bacardi). White rum is bottled immediately after distillation, whereas dark rums are cask-aged, before they are bottled; the longer they are aged, the richer the flavour and deeper the colour. Dark rum is an excellent base for Rumtopf (page 80) and white rum works well with strong-flavoured ingredients such as coffee or spices.

Whisky has a very distinctive flavour which varies between brands. It originated in the Scottish Highlands but is now brewed all around the world. The most highly prized are single malts, produced from malted barley, double-distilled and made at just one distillery (hence the name). Generally, when making liqueurs and flavoured whiskies, you should choose a good quality, but not overly expensive, blended whisky.

Brandy is a grape-based spirit distilled from wine, the most famous of which is cognac, from western France. It makes a great base for liqueurs such as Cherry Brandy (page 52) and Crème de Mure (page 96).

Equipment

While very few specialist items are essential for making cordials, syrups and liqueurs, having the correct equipment for the job will make the whole process easier. You will probably already have most of the basic items such as a large pan, chopping board, wooden spoons, weighing scales and calibrated measuring jugs, but a few specific items such as a funnel and a jelly bag will prove invaluable.

A **large saucepan** is essential. It must be of a sufficient size to hold a good amount of fruit and to allow gentle simmering without boiling over. Ideally it should be wide to allow evaporation of liquid when you want to concentrate cordials, and have a thick heavy base so that you can slowly cook fruit and dissolve sugar. A preserving pan is ideal. It usually has two small handles or a carrying handle over the top, which allows you to pick it up easily and carefully tip out the contents into a sieve or jelly bag. A non-corrosive pan such as one made of stainless steel is the best choice for making cordials and syrups, which are often made with acidic fruit.

Large, wide-necked, sealable glass jars or bottles such as Kilner-type jars are invaluable for steeping cordials and liqueurs until they are ready to be decanted into presentation or storage bottles. Choose ones which have a screw top or clip-top lids with airtight, reusable rubber seals. Most are clear glass, so these should be stored in a dark place while you are steeping flavouring ingredients.

Small plastic bottles with screwtops are ideal for freezing many cordials and syrups. If previously used, these should be washed and air-dried. When filling, don't forget to leave a small space between the cordial and the top of the bottle to allow for expansion as it freezes. Most cordials will keep for 8–9 months if frozen, so that you can enjoy them out of season. Leave to defrost in the fridge overnight.

A **jelly bag** is used to strain fruit juices from cooked fruit pulp and may be made from nylon, calico or cotton flannel. The very close weave allows only the fruit juice to flow through. Some jelly bags have their own stands; others have loops with which to suspend the bag from an upturned stool or chair. Before use, sterilize the jelly bag by scalding in boiling water. This also helps the juices to run through the bag, rather than being absorbed into it. Immediately after use, wash thoroughly, then rinse several times to remove any trace of detergent. Ensure the bag is completely dry before storing; it may be used many times, but make sure you sterilize it before every use.

Muslin, also known as 'cheesecloth', makes a good alternative to a jelly bag and can be used to line a colander or large sieve placed over a bowl. When making very small amounts of cordial or syrup, strain through a disposable **coffee filter.**

A **funnel** makes pouring cordials and syrups into bottles much easier and allows you to direct hot sticky cordials and syrups without the liquid dribbling down the side of the bottle. Choose one with a slimmer tube that will fit into bottles, either made of stainless steel or heat-resistant plastic, rather than a jam funnel.

Use stainless steel, nylon or heat-resistant plastic **sieves and colanders** when straining acidic fruits, as some metals may spoil the colour and give a metallic taste to the finished cordial or syrup. A fine-meshed sieve can often be used instead of a jelly bag or muslin, but may allow very tiny solid particles to pass through. This is fine if you are planning to keep the cordial for just a few weeks.

A **spice ball** is a small, hinged stainless-steel mesh ball, excellent for holding small amounts of spices such as cloves and star anise. These are especially useful if you want to use the leftover fruit purée for dessert-making without having to search for and remove the spices.

Bottles come in all shapes and sizes and various colours. Clear glass allows you to see the colour of the finished cordial, but green ones help you to retain the colour as they filter out light (which is why red wine is stored in green or brown bottles). When making cordials and syrups, it is often better to use several smaller bottles than one large one, as once opened the contents will deteriorate more quickly.

Step-by-step Guide to Making Cordials and Syrups

Most cordials and syrups are made in a similar way: the basic principle is to simmer the fruit, flowers or herbs in a relatively small amount of water to extract the juice or infuse the water, strain and discard the pulp, then sweeten the liquid. Sugar may be added while cooking the fruit or to the strained liquid. This basic technique can be applied to most fruit.

1. Pick the fruit, flowers or herbs and wash if necessary, discarding any that are very over- or under-ripe or damaged. Some fruit, such as apples, pears and nectarines, should be prepared by removing the cores or stones and chopping into smaller pieces so that they will cook more quickly and retain as much of the fresh flavour as possible.

2. Put in a large saucepan with the required amount of water – with berries and very juicy fruit a few spoonfuls of water may be sufficient; with fruit that will need longer cooking, less juicy fruit such as apples, and herbs, where you want to extract the flavour from the leaves, you will need more water. As a very rough guide, add 150ml water per 450g of fruit; with leaves, add enough water so that they are barely covered.

3. Bring to the boil and simmer until tender. Don't cook for longer than is necessary or boil rapidly as this will spoil the flavour and destroy vitamins. You may need to cover the pan so that the fruit gently steams or leave the pan uncovered so that some of the liquid evaporates to make a more concentrated cordial. How much liquid is produced will depend on the type of fruit used, how ripe it is and the weather prior to picking; in very dry weather fruit will be less juicy.

4. Strain the mixture through a jelly bag, fine-meshed sieve or muslin-lined colander over a bowl. Straining the pulp may take a while – several hours or even overnight. With most fruits, the pulp shouldn't be squeezed, as this will make the juice cloudy. Even if you don't mind cloudiness, tiny fruit solids may ferment and affect the length of time the liquid will keep.

5. Return the liquid to the clean pan and add sugar, allowing about 150–350g sugar to 600ml liquid. This will depend on the sweetness of the fruit and personal preference. Slowly bring to the boil, stirring occasionally, until the sugar has dissolved, then bring up to boiling point and simmer for a minute or slightly longer. This ensures that any micro-organisms are destroyed.

6. The cordial may be bottled while hot into warm sterilized bottles, or left to cool and bottled into cold bottles which have been sterilized then allowed to cool. You can then either heat-treat the cordial using the water-bath method (see page 10) or store in a cool dark place, in the fridge or in the freezer (plastic bottles only). All the cordials and syrups and some alcoholic drinks in this book can be drunk straight away, unless the recipe states they should first be matured.

How to Sterilize Glass Bottles

Cordials, syrups and liqueurs can be kept for weeks, months or years as long as the bottles in which they are stored (and bottle tops) are sterilized. Always wash bottles thoroughly first in hot soapy water, and use a bottle brush to thoroughly clean the inside if reusing bottles, then rinse well. It's always a good idea to sterilize one more bottle than you think you'll need. If using any of the first three methods here, allow the bottles to cool very slightly before filling with hot liquid, or to cool completely if filling with cold. Plastic bottles used for freezing cannot be sterilized; they should be washed and rinsed thoroughly and allowed to air-dry.

Dry oven method

This is ideal if you have a lot of large or tall bottles to sterilize. Stand the bottles, spaced slightly apart, on a baking tray. Place in a cold oven and heat to 100°C/fan 80°C/gas ¼. Turn off the oven after 30 minutes. Don't put the bottles into a preheated oven as they may crack. If the tops are plastic, briefly boil them separately.

Boiling water method

This is suitable for smaller bottles. Immerse the bottles open-end up in a deep pan of cold (or lukewarm) water, making sure that they are completely submerged. Bring the water to the boil then boil rapidly for 10 minutes. Add metal, plastic tops or corks for the last minute. Turn off the heat and leave in the pan until the water stops bubbling, then carefully remove the bottles and allow them to drain upside down on a thick clean tea towel; you may need to put this inside a large bowl to balance the bottles and stop them from falling over. Turn the bottles upright and leave to air-dry for a few minutes.

Dishwasher method

Probably the easiest method is to put the bottles in a dishwasher on the hottest setting. This is only suitable for new bottles or used bottles which have previously contained alcohol as the dishwasher will only reach a temperature of 65–70°C. Put the bottles neck-side down in the dishwasher and wash without using a dishwasher tablet or powder on the highest possible setting.

Microwave method

Ideal if you are only sterilizing a few bottles. First make sure that the bottles will fit into the microwave, then half-fill with cold or lukewarm water. Heat on full power until the water has boiled for at least one minute. Using oven gloves, remove the bottles. Holding the bottles over the sink, very carefully swirl the hot water inside them, then tip it away. Drain upside down on a clean tea towel, then turn the bottles upright and leave to air-dry for a few minutes.

Sterilizing tablets

This is unsuitable for delicately flavoured cordials or syrups as it may leave a slight taste behind. Following the instructions on the packet, dissolve the tablets and soak the bottles in the sterilizing solution. Drain well and leave to dry before use.

Water-bath sterilization

If you want to keep your cordials and syrups for up to a year, you will need to sterilize the bottles before filling using any of the above methods, then sterilize again once they have been filled and sealed. Bring the cordial or syrup to just above simmering point (it should reach 90°C on a sugar thermometer), then fill hot bottles to within 3.5cm of the brim. Swing-tops should be sealed and screw tops closed lightly, then tightened after sterilizing. Fill and seal each bottle one at a time. Place a wire trivet or folded tea towel in the bottom of a saucepan (if the bottles touch the bottom of the pan, they may crack) deep enough to submerge the bottles fully. Slowly bring the water to simmering point (88–90°C) and maintain this for 20 minutes. Turn off the heat and leave for a few minutes, then carefully remove the bottles and leave to cool. It's easier to remove the bottles if you scoop out some of the boiling water with a heatproof jug first.

Freezing

Most cordials and syrups can also be frozen (check individual recipes first) in small clean plastic bottles with screw tops. Don't fill completely when freezing; leave about 3cm for the frozen liquid to expand. Label the bottles with freezer-proof labels or a permanent marker pen. This is especially important if you are freezing several different cordials; frozen drinks can look very different from when they are fresh.

Safe Storage

Bottled drinks are best stored in a cool, dark, dry place. If you don't have a cool larder or cupboard, a well-ventilated garage may be an option, but store the drinks in boxes to keep them dust-free and make a note on your calendar, so that you don't forget about them. If you do decide to have your bottled drinks on display, make sure that they are kept out of direct sunlight and be aware that exposure to light will gradually affect their colour and flavour and shorten shelf life. Once opened, drinks with a low or no alcohol content and those with perishable ingredients such as cream should be stored in the fridge.

Chills and Frills: How to Serve

Simple, plain, good-quality glasses are the best way to serve your lovingly made drinks. Coloured and elaborately patterned glasses look great in a display cabinet but can detract from clear-coloured cordials and syrups. Serve in appropriate glasses: tall highball glasses or long-stemmed ones for chilled drinks, so you can hold the glass without warming the drink (or chilling your hand), slim flutes for sparkling drinks like elderflower champagne to keep them fizzy as long as possible, and heavy short glasses for tipples such as blackberry whisky; cut-glass is perfect. For young children sturdy plastic glasses are the most sensible choice, rather than flimsy cardboard cups which are easy to spill. In hot summer weather, lidded cups with straws attract fewer wasps. You can also buy 'party-proof' glassware made from polycarbonate, which looks similar to glass but is unbreakable and ideal for picnics and outdoor dining.

Drinks should always be served at the right temperature; fizzy drinks and most vodka-based tipples are best well chilled. When making long drinks, don't forget to chill mixers as well, and keep plenty of ice in the freezer for those sunny days that may catch you by surprise. Glasses can be chilled in the fridge too, if space allows, for an attractive frosted effect, particularly little shot glasses for liqueurs like Limoncello (page 20), which should be served icy cold. On the other hand, drinks such as Beech Leaf Noyau (page 14) and Blackberry Whisky (page 90) are meant to be drunk at room temperature, so if you store them in an unheated larder, try to remember to take them out an hour or so before serving to allow them to benefit from the warmth of a centrally-heated room.

All the trimmings

Keep garnishes small and subtle unless you are making colourful cocktails or having a Caribbean-themed party, in which case paper umbrellas and mini sparklers would be appropriate and fun, as would sugar-rimmed glasses; dip tall tumblers and cocktail glasses into a saucer of lemon juice then into a saucer of caster sugar. For more classic drinks, stick to 'ice and a slice', whether a sliver of lemon, lime or cucumber or a sprig of fresh mint and a fresh berry or two. Avoid adding masses of chopped fruit and herb leaves to glasses as their flavour can be overpowering and it can make drinks difficult to manage. Floral or fruity ice cubes are an attractive compromise: half-fill large ice-cube compartments with water (boiled water left to cool will make the clearest ice), add fruit or flowers and freeze, then top up with water and freeze again. Try tiny strawberries, blueberries, citrus zest or small rose petals (from unsprayed roses). Alternatively, make ice cubes from the diluted cordials and syrups you are serving and mix and match, for example add a lime cordial cube to a passion fruit drink. Don't try this with liqueurs or neat cordials as alcohol and high sugar mixtures won't freeze solid.

Giving as Gifts

Bottled drinks make gorgeous gifts and it's worth making a little bit more effort to ensure they are beautifully presented. You can of course buy bottles specifically for this purpose, including ones with swing-top ceramic lids for cordials and hip flask-shaped bottles specifically designed for sloe gin, harking back to days gone by. Recycled bottles are fine as long as they are in good condition with no chips or cracks, which might cause the bottle to break during sterilization.

If a bottle still has a faint whiff of its original contents, add a teaspoon of bicarbonate of soda and fill with lukewarm water. Leave for several hours, then tip away and rinse thoroughly. If the drink still contains flavouring ingredients, such as lemon peel or a stick of cinnamon, check to see if it would look better replaced with a fresh piece. No matter how much care you take, bottles often become sticky when filling, so wipe with a damp cloth straight away or you may forget to do so later.

Jazz up bottles with attractive labels tied on with rustic twine or a pretty ribbon and make sure you include information about the contents, including serving suggestions, how to store and a 'use by' date. Alternatively, use metallic glass labelling pens to personalize bottles.

Spring

After winter, the first few blooms and new green leaves are a very welcome sight. Stock up your store-cupboard ingredients if you want to make cordials such as Beech Leaf Noyau or Nettle Syrup as they rely on the youngest of leaves, just unfurled, and if you wait more than a few days you will miss the opportunity of making these. Mint Liqueur and Sage Elixir are other leafy herb drinks to make at this time of year before the leaves become large and tough. If spring is late arriving, make the most of all the citrus fruit available; at this time of year it's at its best and cheapest. Try making St Clement's Cordial, a tasty combination of oranges and lemons, or a bottle of Limoncello, an intensely lemony liqueur from southern Italy. Towards the end of spring, look out for 'forced' new season rhubarb in the shops (if you don't grow your own). It has lovely delicate pink stems and is much sweeter at this time of year; combined with early-season strawberries, it hints at summer months, yet to come.

Beech Leaf Noyau

A noyau is an alcoholic cordial made from gin or brandy, or a mixture of both, flavoured with a slightly bitter agent, often almonds or peach kernels. Although the name *noyau* is a French word, meaning 'nut liqueur', this is a traditional British recipe made with very young beech leaves. It has a lovely flavour, somewhat reminiscent of hazelnuts.

Keeps for 2 years
Makes about 1 litre

Young beech leaves (enough to half-fill a litre jar)
70cl bottle (700ml) gin
250g caster or granulated sugar
250ml water
100ml brandy

1. Strip the beech leaves from their stems and pack into a large clean one-litre Kilner-type jar until it is almost half-full. Pour over the gin, seal the jar and store in a cool dark place for three weeks; the gin will turn a yellowy-green colour and take on a rich nutty scent.
2. Put the sugar and water in a saucepan and gently heat, stirring occasionally, until the sugar has dissolved. Bring to the boil, then turn off the heat and leave to cool.
3. Strain the beech leaf-flavoured gin into the pan through a fine-meshed sieve or a muslin-lined colander, discarding the leaves. Add the brandy and mix well.
4. Pour through a funnel into sterilized bottles and seal. Store in a cool dark place for up to 2 years.

Cook's notes

Only use very young beech leaves, freshly stripped from the stem. The new leaves unfurl around mid-April, although this depends on the weather and location of the tree.

This alcoholic cordial improves as it matures, so store for a few months before sampling. It should keep for up to two years. It can be drunk neat and is traditionally served at room temperature. It also makes an excellent mixer with tonic water or a not-too-sweet ginger ale.

Ginger Syrup

Fresh root ginger is used in this warming syrup, together with a hint of lemon and a few black peppercorns, if liked, which are barely detectable but add a slightly spicy kick. It's fantastic to serve over poached fruit and also good as a soothing hot drink.

Keeps for up to 3 weeks in the fridge, or freeze in small plastic bottles
Makes about 450ml

100g fresh root ginger
1 unwaxed lemon
350g caster or granulated sugar
500ml water
4 black peppercorns (optional)

1. Peel the skin off, then slice or roughly chop the ginger. Thinly pare the rind from the lemon, taking care to avoid the white pith.
2. Put the ginger, lemon rind and sugar in a large saucepan and pour over the water. Gently heat, stirring occasionally, until the sugar has completely dissolved, then bring to the boil.
3. Lower the heat, cover the pan with a lid and simmer for 20 minutes. Add the black peppercorns, if using, and simmer for a further 4–5 minutes.
4. Meanwhile, cut the lemon in half and squeeze out the juice. Add to the pan and simmer for about 30 seconds, then turn off the heat and leave the syrup to cool.
5. Strain the syrup through a fine-meshed sieve or a muslin-lined colander and discard the ginger, lemon rind and peppercorns. Pour into sterilized bottles, seal and store in the fridge, or freeze in small plastic bottles. Serve diluted with hot or cold water.

Cook's notes

This syrup is great added to fresh fruit salad or spooned over steamed sponge puddings or scoops of vanilla ice cream.

If you use powdered cold and flu remedies that are mixed with hot water, add a few tablespoons of this syrup; it will make them a lot more palatable!

Poached Pears

Serves 4

Thinly peel 4 ripe pears, leaving the stalks on. Using a small sharp knife, work up from the base of each pear to make a narrow tunnel and remove the core, keeping the pear whole. Place the pears in a saucepan in which they fit snugly. Sprinkle with 50g soft light brown sugar, then add ½ cinnamon stick and 4 whole cloves, tucking between the pears. Pour over 200ml **ginger syrup**, then add enough boiling water to just cover the pears (the stalks don't need to be covered). Quickly bring to the boil, then turn off the heat and leave the pears to cool in the syrup. Transfer the pears to bowls and serve with some of the syrup spooned over. If liked, you can boil the syrup for a few minutes to reduce and thicken it.

Lemongrass and Ginger Cordial

This fragrant and aromatic cordial makes a great non-alcoholic alternative to the obligatory lager to serve with Indian, Thai or Chinese dishes. It works especially well with those that contain coconut and coriander.

Keeps for 2 weeks
Makes about 450ml

8 lemongrass stalks
Two pieces of fresh root ginger, each about 5 x 3cm
2 fresh limes
200g caster or granulated sugar
500ml water

1. Trim the ends of the lemongrass and peel away the rough outer leaves. Slice lengthways and roughly chop. Bruise by crushing with the back of a tablespoon, then place in a large saucepan.
2. Peel and thinly slice the ginger. Thinly pare the rind from the limes, taking care to avoid the white pith. Add the ginger and lime peel to the lemongrass in the pan along with the sugar, then pour in the water.
3. Gently heat the pan, stirring occasionally, until the sugar has dissolved. Bring to the boil, then lower the heat and simmer uncovered for 5 minutes.
4. Meanwhile, halve the limes and squeeze out the juice. Add to the pan and simmer for just a few more seconds. Turn off the heat, cover the pan with a lid and leave to cool.
5. Strain the mixture through a fine-meshed sieve or muslin-lined colander into a jug, discarding the lemongrass, ginger and lime rind. Pour into sterilized bottles, seal and store in the fridge for up to two weeks.

Cook's notes

Serve this cordial diluted with water to taste or try a mixture of pure apple juice and water.

Stir a few spoonfuls into an 'exotic' fruit salad made from canned lychees and wedges of kiwi fruit – perfect for serving after an Asian meal.

Thai Prawn Stir-fry

Serves 4

Put 1 roughly chopped green chilli, 1 peeled garlic clove, the trimmed stalks from a bunch of fresh coriander, 3 tablespoons fish sauce and 3 tablespoons **lemongrass and ginger cordial** in a small blender or nut grinder. Blend until smooth, then pour over 400g raw peeled tiger prawns and stir to coat. Leave to marinate for a few minutes. Meanwhile, heat 1 tablespoon groundnut oil in a wok or large frying pan. Add 8 sliced spring onions and stir-fry for 1 minute, then add 1 seeded and sliced red pepper and stir-fry for 1 minute. Add 100g sliced water chestnuts and 200g beansprouts and stir-fry for 2–3 minutes until tender. Sprinkle over 2 tablespoons soy sauce. Stir, then tip into a warmed dish. Cover and keep warm.

Heat 1 tablespoon groundnut oil in the wok. Take the prawns out of the marinade and add to the pan. Stir-fry for 2 minutes. Add the marinade and cook for a further minute, or until the prawns are pink and cooked through. Spoon on top of the stir-fried vegetables, garnish with chopped coriander leaves and serve straight away with egg or rice noodles.

Limoncello

In southern Italy this intensely lemony liqueur is served in tiny glasses and sipped chilled as an after-dinner digestif accompanied by crunchy almond biscotti. It is equally delicious served as a long drink with crushed ice and sparkling water.

Keeps for 2 years
Makes about 1 litre

3 unwaxed lemons, plus one for decorating the finished limoncello
500ml vodka (unflavoured)
375g caster sugar
350ml boiling water

1. Thinly pare the rind from the lemons, taking care not to include any of the white pith, which would make the drink slightly bitter. Place the rind in a large, clean, sealable jar, such as a one-litre Kilner jar.
2. Pour over the vodka and close the jar. Leave in cool dark place for a week, giving the jar a gentle shake every day.
3. Put the sugar in a large heatproof bowl or jug and pour over the boiling water. Stir until the sugar has completely dissolved. Stir the lemon vodka into the hot syrup, then pour back into the jar, close the lid and leave for a further week; there's no need to shake the jar daily at this stage.
4. Strain and discard the lemon rind. Pour the limoncello into a sterilized bottle or jar, adding a few fresh strips of lemon rind for decoration. Enjoy straight away or seal and store in a cool dark place for up to two years.

Cook's notes

Limoncello is traditionally made with Sorrento lemons, which have a thick, bumpy, fragrant rind (nearly two-thirds of the fruit grown in this region are made into limoncello). Any good-quality lemons will be fine for making this liqueur, but make sure they are unwaxed and have a bright yellow colour.

If serving as an after-dinner drink, chill both the limoncello and the glasses.

This is delicious drizzled over pancakes (remember to start making at least two weeks before Pancake Day) or poured over scoops of ice cream for a grown-up dessert.

Variation

For orangecello, use the rind from three unwaxed oranges and a strip of lemon rind and make in the same way as limoncello, decorating the bottles with a few fresh strips of orange rind.

Almond Biscotti

Makes 24

These little biscuits are traditionally served with **limoncello**. Spread 75g whole blanched almonds on a baking sheet and toast in the oven at 170°C/fan 160°C/gas 3 for 4–5 minutes or until light golden. Allow to cool, then grind in a nut grinder or food processor until fine. Sift 250g plain flour, 1½ teaspoons baking powder and a pinch of salt into a mixing bowl. Add the finely grated rind of 1 orange or lemon.

Cut 75g butter into small pieces, stir into the flour mixture, then rub in until the mixture resembles breadcrumbs. Stir in 120g caster sugar and the ground nuts. Make a well in the middle and add 1 egg beaten together with 2 tablespoons Amaretto (page 120). Mix together to make a firm dough. Lightly knead on a floured surface for a few seconds until smooth. Shape into two long cylinders each about 6cm wide and place on a baking sheet lined with baking parchment. Bake for 20 minutes until golden around the edges.

Allow to cool slightly, then cut into 1cm thick slices using a sharp knife. Place cut-side down on the baking sheet and bake for a further 8–10 minutes until golden brown and dry to the touch. Cool on a wire rack and store in an airtight tin for up to a week.

Mint Liqueur

Made from fresh mint leaves, 'crème de menthe' makes a great after-dinner liqueur and is especially good served with chocolate desserts. Glycerine gives the drink 'body' and a slightly thicker consistency, but it can be left out if you prefer.

Keeps for 18 months
Makes about 1 litre

75g fresh peppermint or spearmint leaves
750ml vodka (unflavoured)
350g caster or granulated sugar
250ml water
1 tsp glycerine
4–6 drops green food colouring (optional)

1. Rinse the mint leaves and pat dry on kitchen paper. Place in a large, clean, sealable jar, such as a one-litre Kilner jar, and pour over the vodka. Seal the jar and leave in a cool dark place for 3-4 days.
2. Strain the mint-infused vodka through a fine-meshed sieve or a colander lined with muslin. Gently squeeze the mint leaves, extracting as much juice as possible, then discard.
3. Put the sugar and water in a saucepan and gently heat, stirring occasionally, until the sugar has dissolved. Bring to boiling point, then turn off the heat and leave to cool completely.
4. Add the mint-infused vodka and glycerine to the sugar syrup, then add a few drops of green food colouring, if you like. Mix well.
5. Pour through a funnel into sterilized bottles, seal and store in a cool dark place. Use within 18 months of making.

Cook's notes

There are many varieties of mint, but the three main species are spearmint, peppermint and apple mint. Spearmint, also known as garden mint, is the type that you will get if you buy mint from the supermarket; it has a slightly sweeter flavour than peppermint, which is sharper and more pungent. Apple mint is milder with a more subtle flavour, so if you use it for this liqueur, increase the quantity a little.

Many commercially made mint liqueurs are clear and uncoloured; this is preferable if you are planning to use the liqueur in desserts and cooking.

Grasshopper Cocktail

Named after its colour, make this by mixing equal parts of green **mint liqueur** (crème de menthe), Crème de Cacao (page 130) and fresh double cream, shaken with ice in a cocktail shaker and strained into chilled cocktail glasses.

After-dinner Mint Syllabub

Serves 4

Whisk 250g mascarpone, 300ml double cream and 3 tablespoons **mint liqueur** until thick enough to hold soft peaks. Fold in 200g after-dinner chocolate mints, chopped or broken into small pieces. Divide between four glasses or small bowls and chill. Decorate with halved or quartered chocolate mints.

Nettle Syrup

While this may not sound like the most appetising syrup, it is surprisingly good and has a flavour not unlike maple syrup; it's great drizzled over pancakes or a steaming bowl of porridge. For a warm-weather drink, try it diluted with soda water and served over ice. This syrup has a reddish colour, rather than the green you might expect.

Keeps for up to 1 year
Makes about 750ml

750g young nettle leaves
500g caster or granulated sugar
600ml water
Large strip lemon zest, or 2 sprigs of lemon balm
1 bay leaf

1. Pick over the leaves to remove any old or damaged ones, bugs and twigs, then rinse in a colander under cold running water. Leave to drain for a few minutes.
2. Meanwhile, put the sugar and water in a large saucepan and heat, stirring occasionally until the sugar has dissolved.
3. Add the nettle leaves and lemon zest or lemon balm and bay leaf and bring to the boil. Reduce the heat and simmer for 3–4 minutes. Turn off the heat, cover the pan with a lid and leave to cool.
4. Strain the syrup through a fine-meshed sieve or a muslin-lined colander into a large jug, then pour through a funnel into sterilized bottles. Enjoy straight away or seal and store in a cool dark place for up to 1 year.

Cook's notes

Only young, fresh leaves should be collected. Early in the season, around March, you can pick the whole plant, but as they mature, just pick the tips. Don't pick when the flowers start to appear. Gather nettles carefully and wear gloves, such as rubber ones, when picking and preparing, so that you don't get stung.

Often regarded as a 'health tonic' and cold remedy by herbalists, nettles do contain a good amount of vitamin C as well as iron, although the former will be reduced when boiling the nettles.

Mini Pancakes with Nettle Syrup

Serves 4

Sift 120g self-raising white flour into a bowl. Make a hollow in the middle. Whisk together 1 egg, 120ml milk and 3 tablespoons **nettle syrup**. Add to the flour and quickly mix together. Heat 1 tablespoon oil in a large frying pan. When the oil is hot, spoon in enough batter to form two or three pancakes, about 6–7cm in diameter. When bubbles rise to the surface and burst, after 2–3 minutes, turn the pancakes and cook for a further 2–3 minutes or until golden brown. Remove the pancakes from the pan, place on a warm plate and cover with a clean tea towel to keep warm while you cook the remaining batter in batches. Serve the pancakes with extra syrup drizzled over.

Passion Fruit Syrup

This very thick and fragrant syrup is fantastic for drizzling over desserts such as panna cotta and cheesecake, or for adding to drinks and cocktails where you want a concentrated flavour without diluting too much.

Keeps for 4 months
Makes about 300ml

200g caster sugar
100ml water
8 large ripe passion fruit

1. Put the sugar and water in a heavy-based pan and gently heat, stirring occasionally, until the sugar has dissolved. Bring to the boil, then turn off the heat.
2. Halve the passion fruit and scoop out the seeds into a sieve placed over a bowl. Spoon 4 tablespoons of the hot sugar syrup over the seeds, leave for 1 minute, then rub the pulpy juice from the seeds with the back of the tablespoon. Discard the seeds.
3. Bring the sugar syrup back to the boil and boil until it reaches 107°C/225°F on a sugar thermometer, or 'thread stage' (take a small amount of syrup on a teaspoon and drop it from about 5cm above the pan. If it forms a long thread like a spider web, it is ready). Add the passion fruit juice, bring back to the boil and simmer for 1 minute.
4. Allow the syrup to cool for 15 minutes, then carefully pour into hot sterilized bottles and seal while still hot. Leave to cool completely, then store in the fridge for up to four months.

Cook's note

Passion fruit are about the size of an egg and contain crunchy seeds surrounded by an intensely flavoured pulp. The fruits become wrinkled as they ripen, but you should avoid any that are starting to shrivel or feel light for their size.

Passion Fruit Martini

Serves 1

Half-fill a cocktail glass with ice. Add 4 tablespoons gin, followed by 2 tablespoons **passion fruit syrup** and 1 tablespoon lime juice or 2 teaspooons lemon juice (this cuts through the sweetness). Top up the glass to within 1–2 cm of the top with soda water. Serve straight away.

Passion Fruit Posset

Serves 4

This old-fashioned English dessert relies on the acid of the fruit to thicken and set the cream and is traditionally made with lemon juice. This passion fruit version is equally delicious and very quick and simple to make.

Put 50g caster sugar and 450ml double cream in a heavy-based saucepan. Heat gently, stirring occasionally, until the sugar has dissolved. Bring to boiling point and let it bubble quite fiercely for exactly 3 minutes, stirring once or twice if necessary to prevent the mixture from catching on the bottom of the pan or boiling over. Immediately remove the pan from the heat. Mix together 4 tablespoons passion fruit syrup and 1 tablespoon lime juice. Stir into the cream mixture; it will thicken. Leave to cool for 5 minutes, then pour into small ramekins or glasses. Leave to cool completely, then chill for at least 2 hours or until set. Spoon 1 tablespoon of **passion fruit syrup** over the top of each portion before serving.

Peppermint and Lime Cordial

Mint and lime make a great combination, each complementing the flavour of the other, and the lime zest adding a natural green colour to this cordial. This is an excellent way to make the most of the first new pungent sprigs of mint when spring arrives.

Keeps for 3 weeks
Makes about 500ml

5 unwaxed limes
350g caster or granulated sugar
350ml water
About 20 small sprigs of mint

1. Thinly pare the rind from the limes, taking care to avoid the white pith, and put it in a large saucepan with the sugar and water. Slowly bring to the boil, stirring occasionally, until the sugar has completely dissolved. Lower the heat, cover with a lid and simmer for 2–3 minutes.
2. Roughly chop the mint, including the stalks. Add to the syrup, re-cover and simmer for a further 2 minutes. Turn off the heat and leave to cool.
3. Halve the limes and squeeze out the juice. Add to the syrup and stir well.
4. Strain the syrup through a fine-meshed sieve or a muslin-lined colander, then pour through a funnel into sterilized bottles and store in the fridge for up to three weeks or freeze in small plastic bottles. Serve diluted with still or fizzy water, using about one-fifth cordial to four-fifths water.

Variation

For a mint and lemon cordial, use 3 large unwaxed lemons instead of the limes.

Mint Mojito Cocktail

Serves 1

Mojito (rum, sugar, lime juice and mint) is Cuba's signature cocktail and it's really easy to make using this cordial as a base. Half-fill a tall highball or cocktail glass with crushed ice or a few ice cubes. Pour over 3 tablespoons **peppermint and lime cordial** followed by 3 tablespoons white rum such as Bacardi), then top up the glass with soda water. Finish with a slice of lime and a sprig of mint, if liked.

Pink Grapefruit Pick-me-up

This non-alcoholic cordial has a lovely sweet and sharp flavour and is fantastic for serving at breakfast or brunch. Try spooning a little over halved yellow or pink grapefruit to intensify its flavour and to sweeten.

Keeps for up to 2 weeks
Makes about 400ml

6 large 'pink' or 'ruby' grapefruit
250ml water
150g caster or granulated sugar
2 tsp citric acid (see page 3)

1. Pare a large strip of zest from one of the grapefruit and put in a pan with the water, sugar and citric acid.
2. Gently heat, stirring occasionally, until the sugar has dissolved. Bring to the boil, reduce the heat a little, then simmer uncovered for 2–3 minutes. Remove the zest and discard.
3. Halve the six grapefruits and squeeze out the juice. Sieve the juice into the pan and simmer for a further 2–3 minutes. Turn off the heat and leave to cool.
4. Pour into sterilized bottles, seal and store in the fridge for up to two weeks, or freeze in small plastic bottles. Dilute to taste with water.

Cook's notes

For a boozy, adults-only version, add a generous dash of tequila to each glass and top up with soda or sparkling water.

This cordial adds a delicious sweet and sour component to a dressing for drizzling over a salad of duck or prawns. Whisk 4 tablespoons olive or sunflower oil with 1 tablespoon **pink grapefruit cordial**, ½ teaspooon Dijon mustard and 2 teaspoons vinegar (balsamic, wine or sherry).

Variation

This cordial can also be made with yellow grapefruit, but leave out the citric acid.

Pink Grapefruit and Gin Granita

Serves 4

Stir 2–3 tablespoons gin into 300ml **pink grapefruit cordial** (don't add more or less gin; the alcohol stops the granita from freezing rock solid, but too much will prevent it from freezing sufficiently). Pour into a shallow freezerproof container and freeze for 6 hours or overnight. Mash with a fork to break up the ice crystals. Return to the freezer until ready to serve spooned into small, chilled glasses.

Rhubarb and Strawberry Vodka

This fruit-infused vodka is the delicate pink colour of spring rhubarb and early-season strawberries. The combination of sweet and sharp makes this a refreshing drink for those first warm and sunny days of the year.

Keeps for 1 year
Makes about 750ml

300g forced rhubarb (pale-pink thin-stemmed variety)
200g medium-sized firm ripe strawberries
300g caster sugar
70cl bottle (700ml) vodka (unflavoured)

1. Trim the rhubarb stems, then wash and dry on kitchen paper. Cut into short lengths, about 2.5cm. Hull the strawberries and rinse if necessary, then pat dry. Cut each strawberry in half.
2. Put the fruit in a large, clean, sealable jar, such as a one-litre Kilner jar, layering the fruit with the sugar. Pour over the vodka, then shake the jar gently.
3. Store in a cool dark place for three to four weeks. Gently shake daily for the first week, to dissolve the sugar, then a couple of times a week.
4. Pour the fruit-infused vodka through a fine-meshed sieve or muslin-lined colander over a bowl. Transfer to a jug and pour carefully into sterilized bottles.
5. The vodka is now ready to drink, or can be stored in a cool dark place for up to a year. Chill in the fridge before serving.

Cook's notes

Serve the vodka over ice or neat in chilled shot glasses. You can chill the vodka in the freezer but only leave it for an hour or two. It's also good in a tall glass, topped with soda water and garnished with fresh strawberry slices.

Don't throw the fruit away; it can be made into a boozy compote by gently cooking in a saucepan with a couple of tablespoons of sugar and a splash of water until the rhubarb is very tender.

Sage Elixir

An elixir is a clear syrup, often medicinal. This bright green one is made from fresh sage leaves steeped in alcohol and is considered to be a health tonic with healing properties. Whether this is true or not, it makes an excellent after-dinner digestif and is also good served in a tall glass with ice and tonic water.

Keeps for up to 1 year
Makes about 400ml

30g fresh sage leaves
250ml eau de vie
100g caster sugar
100ml water

1. Check the leaves for any insects, then pack them into a large, clean, sealable Kilner-type jar with a capacity of around 300ml. Pour over the alcohol, filling to the top, and close the lid. Make sure that all the leaves are covered with alcohol or they will turn brown and discolour the elixir.
2. Leave the jar on a windowsill, but not in direct sunlight, for four weeks, gently shaking the jar every few days.
3. Put the sugar and water in a saucepan and gently heat, stirring occasionally, until the sugar has completely dissolved. Bring to the boil and simmer for 1 minute. Turn off the heat and leave the syrup to cool.
4. Strain the sage-infused alcohol through a fine-meshed sieve or muslin-lined colander into a large jug. Stir in the syrup, then pour into sterilized bottles and seal. Store in a dark cool place. The elixir may be used straight away and will keep for up to a year.

Cook's notes

Although sage is an evergreen, this elixir is best made from young leaves picked between mid-spring and early summer. Pick the leaves on a dry sunny day and use straight away.

Eau de vie is a clear, colourless alcohol. If you prefer, vodka or gin may be used instead.

This elixir is also good made using a mixture of sage and lemon (or regular) thyme.

Try adding a couple of teaspoons of this elixir to sauces or gravy to accompany chicken or duck to add a subtle, sweet, herby flavour.

Spring Rhubarb and Ginger Syrup

Tender pink 'forced' rhubarb is available in very early spring and has a more delicate, less acidic flavour than maincrop rhubarb and makes a lovely 'candy floss' pink-coloured syrup. You can use maincrop rhubarb in this recipe if you prefer, adding a little more sugar and leaving out the lemon juice.

Keeps for up to 2 weeks
Makes about ½ litre

8 stems forced rhubarb
5cm piece fresh root ginger, peeled and cut into 4 pieces
250g caster sugar
150ml water
2 tsp lemon juice

1. Trim and wash the rhubarb and cut into 2cm lengths. Put into a large, non-aluminium heavy-based pan with the ginger, sugar and water.
2. Heat gently, stirring occasionally, until the sugar has completely dissolved. Turn up the heat a little, cover the pan and simmer for 15 minutes or until the rhubarb is very tender and falling apart.
3. Turn off the heat and stir in the lemon juice. Leave to cool for 15 minutes.
4. Tip the rhubarb into a muslin-lined colander over a bowl and leave to drain for several hours. Don't squeeze out the juice or the syrup may be cloudy.
5. Pour the syrup into sterilized bottles, seal and store in the fridge for up to two weeks or freeze in small plastic bottles. Serve diluted, using 1 part syrup to 3 parts water.

Cook's notes

'Forced' rhubarb is more expensive than maincrop rhubarb, but if you grow your own, you can produce it simply by trimming off the leaves and pale pink root slivers at the base of the rhubarb stalks.

Enjoy this syrup as a long drink with a dash of vodka and topped up with soda water.

Variations

For rhubarb and orange syrup, add the pared rind of 1 orange instead of the ginger. Halve the orange, squeeze out the juice and add to the syrup instead of the lemon juice.

For rhubarb and rose water syrup, leave out the ginger and add 2 tablespoons rose water to the cooled syrup before bottling.

Rhubarb and Ginger Ice Cream

Serves 4

Don't waste the rhubarb pulp after draining. Remove the four pieces of ginger and fold the rhubarb into 300ml double cream, whipped to form very soft peaks with 2 tablespoons sifted icing sugar. You can also fold in some finely chopped stem ginger preserved in syrup, if you like. Freeze in a shallow container, whisking 2 or 3 times during freezing to break down the ice crystals. Alternatively, pour into an ice-cream maker and churn until frozen. Allow the ice cream to soften slightly in the fridge or at room temperature before serving.

St Clement's Cordial

'Oranges and lemons say the bells of St. Clement's...' and just like the nursery rhyme, this cordial has a lovely old-fashioned flavour. As oranges on their own can make an overly sweet syrup, adding a lemon and a little citric acid offsets this and enhances the flavour to make a lovely refreshing drink.

Keeps for up to 6 weeks
Makes about 400ml

5 large unwaxed oranges
1 unwaxed lemon
200ml water
100g caster or granulated sugar
1 tsp citric acid (see page 3)

1. Thinly pare the rind from two of the oranges and from half the lemon. Put in a large pan with the water, sugar and citric acid.
2. Slowly bring to the boil, stirring occasionally until the sugar has dissolved. Bring to the boil and simmer for 2–3 minutes.
3. Meanwhile, halve all the fruit and squeeze out the juice into a jug. Add to the pan and gently simmer for a further 5 minutes. Turn off the heat, cover the pan with a lid and leave to cool.
4. Strain the syrup through a fine-meshed sieve back into the jug, discarding the orange and lemon rind. Pour into sterilized bottles and store in the fridge for up to six weeks, or freeze in small plastic bottles. Serve diluted to taste.

> ### Cook's note
> Avoid cooking acidic fruits in aluminium pans (anodized aluminium is fine), as the metal will react with the acid and may be harmful to health.

Boodle's Fool

Serves 4

This famous dish is still served at Boodle's gentlemen's club, which was founded in London over 250 years ago. It is traditionally made with orange and lemon zest and juice, but using this cordial makes it really quick and easy to prepare.

Cut four trifle sponges into 1cm slices and use to line the bottom and halfway up the sides of four individual serving dishes or glasses. Drizzle 1 tablespoon of St Clement's Cordial over each portion. Whip 300ml double cream with 1 tablespoon sifted icing sugar until it just starts to thicken, then slowly add 4 tablespoons cordial, continuing to whip the cream as you do so. Pour over the sponges and chill for at least 2 hours to allow the sponges to moisten and the cream to thicken. Serve decorated with fresh orange segments.

Vanilla Vodka

This very simple recipe has just two ingredients and only takes a few minutes to make, but produces a delicate and fragrant drink that can be enjoyed neat poured over ice, or as an addition to cocktails and desserts.

Keeps for 2–3 years
Makes 500ml

500ml vodka
2 vanilla pods

1. Pour the vodka into a bottle or glass jar (or leave in its bottle if it is the right amount).
2. Split the vanilla pods by cutting in half lengthways. Add to the vodka.
3. Put the cap on the bottle and leave in a cool dark place for four weeks (or longer if you prefer; see Cook's notes). Give the bottle a gentle shake every couple of days for the first week; the vodka will turn a golden colour and will gradually darken a little more over time.

Cook's notes

The vanilla will continue to impart flavour for several months, but when you are happy with the level of vanilla flavour, remove the pods.

Don't leave the pods in the vodka for longer than six months, as they will eventually start to fall apart. You should remove the pods when the vodka no longer covers them, or alternatively you can just top up the bottle with more vodka to replenish. Tiny black vanilla seeds will start to fall out of the pods as soon as they are added to the vodka and they will settle at the bottom of the bottle; if you wish to remove these, filter or strain the infused vodka through a muslin-lined sieve or coffee filter.

Don't throw away the vanilla pods. If they are still in good condition, leave to dry then store in an airtight jar. They can be used in baking and dessert making.

Milky Way Martini

Serves 1

Put a few cubes of ice in a cocktail shaker and pour in 2 tablespoons **vanilla vodka**, 2 tablespoons Crème de Cacao (page 130) and 1 tablespoon Irish Cream Liqueur (page 136). Shake together and pour into a glass. Serve straight away.

Wildflower Syrup

The heady scent of wild flowers can be captured using this simple method in which the flowers are layered with sugar and left for a day to infuse. Take care not to boil the final syrup or you may lose the delicate flavour.

Keeps for 1 year
Makes about 500ml

Enough freshly picked blossoms to reach 500ml in a measuring jug (see Cook's note)
About 500g caster sugar
About 300ml near-boiling water

1. Check the flowers and give them a gentle shake to remove any dust, then remove the petals or sprigs of flowers.
2. Sprinkle a thin layer of sugar in the base of a large, sealable jar, such as a one-litre Kilner jar, then add a layer of petals or flowers, then another layer of sugar. Try to make each layer of sugar or petals as thin as possible, preferably no more than 1cm deep.
3. Continue layering the flowers and sugar until all the flowers are used up, finishing with a layer of sugar. Make a note of how much sugar you have used.
4. Close the jar and leave at room temperature, out of direct sunlight, for 24–36 hours.
5. Empty the sugar and petals into a large saucepan and pour over 60ml of near-boiling water for every 100g sugar you have used (use a little less water if the sugar has become very damp and sticky; this will depend on the type of flowers you have used).
6. Gently heat the mixture, stirring occasionally, until the sugar has completely dissolved. Turn off the heat, cover and leave to cool.
7. Strain the syrup through a fine-meshed sieve or muslin-lined colander, pour into sterilized bottles and seal. Store in a cool dark place. With time, the scent and flavour will decrease, so this syrup is best used within a few months of making, although it will keep for up to one year.

Cook's note

Make sure the flowers you choose are edible and unsprayed. Wild rose, hawthorn and dandelion all work well. You can also use garden flowers such as jasmine, honeysuckle and hibiscus.

Wildflower Icing

Makes enough to cover the top of one large cake (or 12–16 small cakes)

Sift 200g icing sugar into a bowl. Make a hollow in the middle and add 2 tablespoons **wildflower syrup** and a drop of food colouring, if liked. Using a wooden spoon, gradually mix in the syrup, adding a little more syrup if necessary to make a smooth, thick icing with the consistency of thick cream. Use straight away. Decorate the cake(s) with crystallized or icing flowers before the icing sets.

Summer

Here comes summer and no matter what the weather brings, flowers continue to bloom and fruit to ripen. Use the longer and cooler evenings to fill your house with the floral fragrance of Rose Petal or Lavender-scented Syrup. Elderflowers make an appearance early in summer and of all cordials elderflower is probably the best known. Try your hand at making Elderflower Champagne as well; it's a perfect ice-breaker for summer parties and barbecues.

As the summer heats up, cool down with long chilled drinks of Blackcurrant Cordial and fresh child-friendly Cherryade and fizzy Ginger Beer. Summer fruit is plentiful and this is the time to make the most of gluts of soft fruit such as gooseberries, redcurrants, raspberries and strawberries. Before the end of the season, start a Rumtopf. Kick off with strawberries and continue adding different varieties of fruit as they come into season.

Blackcurrant Cordial

Blackcurrants are intensely flavoured and richly coloured berries and as most of the fruit ripens at the same time, you often end up with a glut if you grow your own. If you've ever wondered about the name 'Ribena', it comes from the Latin word for blackcurrants, *ribes*.

Keeps for 3 months
Makes about 600ml

500g blackcurrants
250g caster sugar
250ml water
1 unwaxed lemon

1. Wash the blackcurrants, then remove from the stalks (don't worry if a few tiny stalks remain as you will be sieving later).
2. Put the fruit in a large saucepan with the sugar and about half of the water. Heat, stirring occasionally, until the sugar has dissolved, then bring to the boil and gently simmer for 3–4 minutes.
3. Meanwhile, thinly pare the rind from the lemon, avoiding any white pith. Halve the lemon and squeeze out the juice. Add the rind and juice to the pan and simmer for a further 5 minutes; do not boil vigorously, or you will lose the fresh flavour of the fruit. Turn off the heat and leave to cool for 5 minutes.
4. Carefully pour the fruit and juices into a muslin-lined sieve over a large bowl. Leave to drain for a few minutes, then squeeze out the juices by pushing with the back of a spoon.
5. Tip the fruit pulp back into the pan and stir in the rest of the water. Sieve again to remove the last of the juice and pulp from the seeds.
6. Clean the pan, then return the syrup to the pan and boil for 1 minute. Pour into small hot sterilized bottles and seal in a cool dark place. The cordial will keep unopened for up to three months. Once opened, store in the fridge.

Cook's notes

Serve the cordial diluted with still or sparkling water. It is also delicious with Prosecco or a dry sparkling wine to make a less alcoholic version of Kir Royale.

You can also make this cordial with redcurrants. These tend to be sharper than blackcurrants, so leave out the lemon rind and juice.

Try adding a spoonful or two to enrich gravy or sauces to serve with game or duck.

For a topping sauce for rich plain cheesecakes and similar desserts, simmer 150ml cordial until reduced by about half. Spoon over the top of the cheesecake when the syrup is just cool, then chill the cheesecake; the syrup should thicken further to a lightly set, jelly-like topping.

Cherryade

Most cordials are strained to give a clear syrup, but here the whole fruit is puréed to make a delicious wholesome drink. This version will only keep for a few days in the fridge, but you can freeze it if you want to keep for longer.

Keeps for 3–4 days
Makes 200ml

250g fresh cherries
5 tbsp caster sugar
3 tbsp water
½ tsp vanilla extract

1. Remove the stalks and wash the cherries. Chop each one in half and remove the stones, or do this with a cherry stoner.
2. Put the cherries in a pan with the sugar and water. Slowly bring to the boil, stirring occasionally until the sugar has completely dissolved.
3. Bring to the boil, then lower the heat, cover the pan with a lid and simmer gently for 12–15 minutes or until the fruit is very soft. Turn off the heat and leave to cool for 15 minutes.
4. Add the vanilla extract to the fruit, then tip the mixture into a blender and purée until very smooth. Pour into a jug, leave to cool, then chill in the fridge until ready to serve.
5. Add 4–5 tablespoons of the cherry purée to a glass and add a little chilled fizzy water. Stir well, then top up the glass with more fizzy water and briefly stir again to mix. Serve straight away and store the remainder in the fridge for 3–4 days.

Cook's notes

Cherryade was traditionally made with a sprig of fresh tarragon, which adds a hint of aniseed flavour. If you want to try this, add a sprig of fresh tarragon with the cherries in the pan and remove before puréeing. Leave out the vanilla extract.

Variation

While fresh cherries have a much better flavour, you can make this using a can of cherries. Drain a 425g can of pitted black cherries in light syrup or fruit juice, reserving 6 tablespoons of the syrup. Put the fruit and reserved syrup in a pan with 4 tablespoons caster sugar, heat gently until the sugar has dissolved, then simmer uncovered for 5 minutes until the fruit is very soft and the liquid slightly reduced. Continue as main recipe.

Cherry Bounce

This cherry liqueur originated in the English hamlet of Frithsden and the recipe was taken to America by the Pilgrims in the seventeenth century. A spicy version, similar to this one, is credited to George Washington's wife Martha, the first 'First Lady'. Her recipe contained brandy, but in the deep South, Cherry Bounce was more often made with whisky (as here) or rum, which was cheap and plentiful at that time.

Keeps for 1 year
Makes about 600ml

600g ripe cherries
225g caster sugar
4 whole allspice
4 whole cloves
1 cinnamon stick
600ml whisky

1. Remove the cherries from their stalks, wash and pat dry on kitchen paper. Cut each cherry open with a knife to expose the stone, but don't remove it, and put into a large, clean, sealable jar, such as a one-litre Kilner jar.
2. Sprinkle the sugar over the fruit, close the lid and leave for 1 hour; this will start to draw the juices from the fruit. Add the allspice, cloves and cinnamon stick and pour over the whisky. Seal the jar and shake gently.
3. Leave to steep for eight weeks, giving the jar a gentle shake occasionally for the first week to help dissolve the sugar and blend the flavours.
4. Strain the cherry-infused whisky through a fine-meshed sieve or muslin-lined colander into a bowl, discarding the cherries and spices. Pour the cherry bounce into a jug, then decant into sterilized bottles and seal. This drink is best enjoyed after 2 months' maturing

Cook's notes

Use ripe firm cherries for this liqueur, discarding any that are slightly bruised as they will spoil the flavour.

This is an excellent alternative to brandy, rum or whisky for soaking the dried fruit used to make a rich fruit cake, as it has a lovely, subtle spiced flavour.

Made with either white or dark rum, this makes a fantastic pouring syrup to serve with rum babas filled with summer berries or autumn fruit.

Cherry Cranachan

Serves 4

Typically made with neat whisky and fresh raspberries, this Scottish dessert is good made with **cherry bounce** and a mixture of fresh fruit. Put 75g porridge oats in a large non-stick frying pan and dry-fry over a medium heat for 2 minutes. Add 25g flaked almonds and cook for a further 2–3 minutes, stirring frequently until light golden brown. Remove from the heat and leave to cool. Pour 300ml double cream and 150ml crème fraîche into a bowl. Add 6 tablespoons cherry bounce and 2 tablespoons clear honey. Whisk until floppy peaks form. Fold in two-thirds of the oat and almond mixture. Divide 150g fresh raspberries and stoned cherries between four glasses, then spoon over the oat and cream mixture. Sprinkle over the rest of the oat and almond mixture, decorate with some more fruit and serve straight away.

Cherry Brandy

Make this rich deep-red-coloured brandy drink during the summer when cherries are at their peak and it will be ready for drinking during the first chilly autumn weather. It tastes even better if kept for Christmas.

Keeps for 1 year
Makes about 750ml

300g fresh red cherries
1 tbsp caster sugar
1 cinnamon stick
70cl bottle (700ml) brandy

1. Remove the cherries from their stalks, wash and pat dry on kitchen paper. Cut each cherry open with a knife to expose the stone, but don't remove it (this gives an almondy flavour to the brandy), and put into a sterilized jar.
2. Sprinkle the sugar over the fruit, close the lid and leave for 1 hour; this will start to draw the juices from the fruit.
3. Add the cinnamon stick and pour over the brandy. Seal the jar and shake gently. Leave to steep for eight weeks, giving the jar an occasional gentle shake.
4. Strain the cherry-infused brandy through a sieve, then pour the cherry brandy into clean bottles through a funnel. Use within 1 year of making.

Cook's notes

Substitute vodka for brandy to make cherry schnapps.

Don't discard the cherries; they are fantastic roughly chopped and added to a rich fruit cake instead of some of the dried fruit. Don't forget to remove the cherry stones before chopping.

Singapore Sling

Serves 1

This classic long, fruity cocktail was created around 1910 at the Raffles hotel in Singapore by bartender Mr Ngiam Tong Boon as a 'ladies drink'. Sadly the original recipe was lost in the 1930s. This version is very similar to the drink currently served in Raffles' 'Long Bar'. Pour 120ml pineapple juice, 2 tablespoons gin, 1 tablespoon **cherry brandy**, 1 tablespoon lime juice, ½ tablespoon Cointreau, ½ tablespoon Bénédictine liqueur, 2 teaspoons grenadine and a dash of Angostura bitters into a cocktail shaker. Shake briefly, then serve with ice and decorate the glass with a thin slice of pineapple and a cherry.

Crème de Cassis

The prefix 'crème de' is nothing to do with cream-based liqueurs: it was originally used to distinguish sweetened liqueurs from dry spirits such as cognac. These types of liqueurs usually have just one dominant flavour, often fruit. Crème de Cassis was first made in Burgundy and the famous aperitifs, Kir and Kir Royale, were named after the mayor of Dijon at that time.

Keeps for 2 years
Makes about 1 litre

500g blackcurrants
70cl bottle (700ml) red wine
500g caster sugar
250ml unflavoured vodka

1. Wash the blackcurrants well, then use the tines of a fork to remove them from their sprigs (it doesn't matter if a few tiny sprigs go in as the mixture will be strained later), Put them in a large glass bowl and crush them lightly with a potato masher until all the berries have burst.
2. Pour the wine over the blackcurrants, stir well, then cover and leave to steep at room temperature for 36–48 hours (in very warm weather, 24 hours will be sufficient).
3. Tip through a fine-meshed sieve or muslin-lined colander into a deep clean bowl and leave to drain; this can take several hours. Gently squeeze out the last of the juice through the muslin.
4. Pour the blackcurrant juice and wine mixture into a large saucepan. Add the sugar and gently heat, stirring occasionally, until the sugar has completely dissolved. Leave over a gentle heat for about an hour, so that the liquid reduces a little. It should be just below simmering point; don't allow the mixture to boil. Stir now and then to help evaporation. Turn off the heat and leave to cool.
5. Stir in the vodka, then pour into sterilized bottles. Leave to mature for at least six months in a cool dark place; it should keep for at least two years.

Cook's notes

It's important to use a good 'fresh' (not one that's been stored away for several years) red wine such as fruity Merlot for this recipe.

This is delicious drizzled over cheesecakes, ice cream, fresh fruit or meringue baskets filled with whipped cream and red berries, or follow the French example and serve over cubes of ripe melon.

Its sweet yet slightly acidic taste is also good added to sauces served with rich meat, such as game or pork.

Kir

Serves 1

Pour about 2 teaspoons **crème de cassis** into a wine glass and top with a light, dry white wine, preferably one which is slightly acidic (traditionally Kir is made with a young Bourgogne aligoté). Top crème de cassis with non-vintage brut champagne or a dry sparkling white wine and the drink becomes a Kir Royale.

Elderflower Champagne

The elderflower season heralds the start of summer and the blossoms can continue until the middle of July. When collecting them, try to cut a few sprays from each tree, rather than stripping one bare, so that there will be elderberries later in the year. This fresh and fragrant fizzy beverage is mildly alcoholic with a lovely pale golden colour. It's simple to make, although you need to take a little care when storing.

Keeps for 3 months
Makes about 4 litres

1 unwaxed lemon
600g caster sugar
4 litres cold water
20 heads of elderflower
1½ tbsp white wine vinegar

1. Thinly pare the rind from the lemon, avoiding the white pith, then cut the lemon in half and squeeze out the juice. Put the lemon rind, sugar and 1 litre of the water in a saucepan and gently heat, stirring occasionally, until the sugar has dissolved. Turn off the heat and leave to cool.
2. Meanwhile, give the elderflower heads a shake to remove any dust or insects, then cut off the larger pieces of stalk (too much stalk can make the brew bitter), leaving just the floral sprigs. Put the heads into a very large bowl, stainless steel pan or an immaculately clean food-grade plastic bucket.
3. Pour over the sugar syrup, then add the remaining water, lemon juice and vinegar. Stir gently. Cover tightly with a clean cloth or tea towel and leave to steep.
4. After two days, the mixture should start to ferment. You should see small bubbles appearing on the surface; if not, check again after three days and follow the tip in the cook's note box if necessary. After six days, strain the mixture through a muslin-lined colander and decant into plastic fizzy

pop bottles with screw-top lids, leaving a space of about 3cm at the top for expansion. Store in a cool dark place.

5. Every couple of days (daily if the weather is very warm), check the bottles. If they look as if they are expanding or feel 'tight' when gently squeezed, carefully loosen the caps to allow a little of the gas to escape, then re-tighten. You can drink the champagne after a couple of weeks (chill well first), although it will improve if kept for a month or two. Ideally drink within three months of making. Remember to open the bottles carefully when serving, always pointing the bottle away from yourself (and others).

Cook's notes

Choose creamy-coloured elderflowers that are fully opened but still very fresh, and try to pick early on a sunny day (after the dew has dried) to ensure there is plenty of wild yeast on the flowers. Pick the elderflowers just before you are planning to use them, as, like most wild flowers, they wilt quickly. If you can't use them on the same day, the flowers can be frozen (although they take up a lot of freezer space), but they are better used fresh.

If there are no signs of fermentation after three days, add a pinch of dried yeast, stir well and wait a little longer.

A sediment will form at the bottom of the bottles; this is perfectly normal. Either pour very carefully, or decant the elderflower champagne into a chilled jug just before serving.

It's essential to check the bottles regularly as the 'champagne' will continue to produce carbon dioxide, which, if left, may cause the bottles to split or even explode.

Elderflower Cordial

As the flowers are only around for a month or two, it's worth freezing some of this cordial for later in the year to remind you of summer. Citric acid is a natural preservative and adds a refreshing tang to the drink.

Keeps for 2–3 weeks
Makes about 2 litres

1.5kg granulated sugar
1.5 litres boiling water
30 elderflower heads
2 unwaxed lemons, thinly sliced
2 unwaxed limes, thinly sliced
1½ tbsp citric acid (see page 3)

1. Put the sugar and water in a saucepan and gently heat, stirring occasionally, until the sugar has completely dissolved. Turn off the heat.
2. Meanwhile, give the elderflower heads a shake to remove any dust or insects, then cut off the larger pieces of stalk (too much stalk can make the cordial bitter) leaving just the floral sprigs. Briefly rinse them in a bowl of cold water, then shake off the excess water.
3. Put the elderflowers and lemon and lime slices in a large bowl and pour over the hot syrup (it should be fairly warm, but if it is steaming hot, let it cool a little first). Add the citric acid and stir well. Cover the bowl with a clean cloth and leave to steep at room temperature for 24–36 hours.
4. Strain the cordial through a fine-meshed sieve or a colander lined with muslin, then pour into sterilized bottles and seal. It will keep for two to three weeks in a cool, dark place (preferably a fridge, if space allows). If you would like to keep it for up to a year, follow the water-bath sterilization method (see page 10). Alternatively, freeze in small plastic bottles.

Cook's notes

Serve elderflower cordial diluted with still or sparkling water and ice. It's also a good non-alcoholic alternative to gin when served with tonic water and is delicious with ginger ale.

Many recipes for elderflower cordial contain just lemons, but limes add a subtler flavour and a slightly greener colour. If you prefer, use an extra lemon instead of the two limes.

Gooseberry and Elderflower Fool

Serves 4

Wash 100g gooseberries, then top and tail using a small sharp knife. Put in a saucepan with 2 tablespoons water and bring to the boil. Reduce the heat and cook gently for 12–15 minutes until softened to a thick purée. Turn off the heat and stir in 3 tablespoons **elderflower cordial**. Tip into a bowl, leave to cool, then chill in the fridge for 1 hour. Whip 300ml double cream and 1 tablespoon icing sugar together to form very soft peaks. Gently fold in the gooseberry mixture, leaving it slightly marbled. Spoon into four dessert dishes and decorate with mint sprigs just before serving.

Ginger Beer

Although fresh ginger is available all year round, this drink is synonymous with summer picnic fare and is well known for being the favourite drink of Enid Blyton's 'Famous Five'. As with Elderflower Champagne (page 56), care needs to be taken when making this fizzy brew.

Keeps for 2 weeks
Makes 2 litres

2 tbsp peeled and grated fresh root ginger
200g granulated sugar
½ tsp cream of tartar
1 unwaxed lemon
2 litres cold water
½ tsp fast-action dried yeast

1. Put the ginger, sugar and cream of tartar in a large saucepan. Peel off a small strip of rind from the lemon (this will add just a hint of flavour), then cut the lemon in half and squeeze out the juice. Add the rind and juice to the pan. Pour over about 500ml of the water.

2. Gently heat, stirring occasionally, until the sugar has dissolved, then bring to the boil and gently simmer uncovered for 5 minutes. Turn off the heat, cover the pan with a lid and leave to cool for 10 minutes to allow the ginger and lemon to infuse.

3. Add the rest of the water; the mixture should be tepid. Sprinkle the yeast over the surface, stir well, then cover with the lid and leave for 3–4 hours.

4. Strain the liquid through a fine-meshed sieve into a jug, then pour into two one-litre clean plastic soft drink bottles, leaving a 3cm gap at the top. Make sure you divide the thick yeasty mixture at the bottom evenly between the bottles.

5. Screw on the bottle tops and leave in a cool dark place for three days, loosening the bottle tops every day (twice a day in very warm weather) to release the pressure of carbon

dioxide. The ginger beer will then be ready to drink. If you keep it for longer, continue checking the bottles daily, loosening the tops if the bottles feel very tight when lightly (and carefully!) squeezed.

6. Store in the fridge for up to two weeks and remember to open the bottles carefully when serving, always pointing the bottle away from yourself (and others). Serve chilled or over ice.

Cook's notes

Never use glass bottles when making ginger beer as they may shatter.

Once made, ginger beer doesn't keep for very long. It becomes less sweet as the yeast continues to use the sugar to make carbon dioxide – the gas that makes the drink fizzy, so serve within a week or two of making.

Gooseberry and Elderflower Syrup

Pale green gooseberries and fragrant elderflowers make perfect partners in this fruity aromatic syrup, which will turn a beautiful deep pink colour during cooking. Use the syrup to flavour ice creams, sorbets and fruit salads, and to moisten gooseberries in a pie or crumble.

Keeps for 8 weeks
Makes about 500ml

450g granulated sugar
250ml water
650g young sharp gooseberries
4 heads of elderflowers
1 tbsp lemon juice

1. Put the sugar and water in a large saucepan and gently heat, stirring occasionally, until the sugar has dissolved.
2. Add the gooseberries and slowly bring to the boil. Turn down the heat until the mixture is barely simmering, half-cover the pan with a lid and cook for 10 minutes.
3. Rinse the elderflowers in cold water, then pick the tiny groups of flowers off the larger stems. Add to the gooseberries with the lemon juice, re-cover the pan and cook for a further 10 minutes. Turn off the heat and leave to cool.
4. Strain though a fine-meshed sieve or a muslin-lined colander into a large jug. Pour into sterilized bottles, seal and store in a cool dark place. Use within eight weeks of making.

Cook's notes

While gooseberries are a native plant throughout northern Europe, they are really only cultivated in Britain (mainly in the East and South-Eastern counties.) While sweeter red 'dessert' varieties are usually eaten raw, the traditional green acidic ones are better cooked and are ideal for this syrup.

If you want to use the leftover gooseberry pulp for gooseberry fool, ice creams, etc, enclose the elderflowers in a piece of tied muslin before adding to the gooseberries, so that it can easily be removed.

Lavender Lemonade

It's fun to watch this fragrant floral drink turn a beautiful pale pink colour when the lemon juice is added. It's best made from lavender just past its peak and starting to dry. Leave any newly opened flowers for the bees to enjoy.

Keeps for 3–4 weeks
Makes about 1.5 litres

10–15g lavender heads
4 unwaxed lemons
100g caster sugar
500ml boiling water
3 tbsp clear honey
1 litre cold water

1. Give the lavender a good shake to remove any dust or insects, then put the flower heads into a saucepan.
2. Thinly pare a strip of rind from one of the lemons and add to the pan with the sugar. Pour over the boiling water. Bring to the boil and simmer for 1 minute, then turn off the heat, cover the pan with a lid and leave until tepid.
3. Stir in the honey, then add the cold water. Halve the lemons and squeeze out the juice. Add to the pan.
4. Strain through a muslin-lined sieve into a large jug and leave to cool, then chill in the fridge. Serve poured over ice and diluted with a little more water if needed.

Cook's notes

Serve as an alternative to hot tea at an afternoon tea party. It's perfect with dainty cakes such as pastel-coloured fondant fancies or tiny cupcakes.

Use an ordinary honey for this drink, as delicately flavoured ones will be overpowered by the lemon flavour. If you prefer, you can use an extra 25g caster sugar instead of honey.

Lavender-scented Syrup

Use this highly scented flowery syrup sparingly in cooking. It is lovely with fresh juicy peaches or raspberries and perfect for flavouring cakes and whipped cream, adding a subtle purplish-pink colour.

Keeps for 1 month
Makes about 150ml

About 10 heads of lavender or 3 tbsp dried lavender
1 unwaxed lemon
200g caster sugar
150ml water

1. Give the lavender a good shake to remove any dust or insects, then put the flower heads or dried lavender into a saucepan.
2. Thinly pare a strip of rind from the lemon, taking care to avoid the white pith, and put in the pan with the sugar. Halve the lemon and squeeze out the juice. Add to the pan with the water. Bring to the boil, stirring occasionally until the sugar has dissolved.
3. Simmer uncovered for 5 minutes, until the syrup is slightly reduced, then turn off the heat, cover the pan with a lid and leave to cool.
4. Strain through a fine-meshed sieve or muslin-lined colander and store in a bottle in the fridge for up to a month.

> ### Cook's notes
>
> Flowers for this syrup should be picked in early summer. There are many different types of lavender and some are more suitable for culinary use than others, so choose carefully.
>
> Place freshly picked lavender on kitchen paper for a few hours to allow it to dry slightly.
>
> Add a tablespoon of lavender syrup to a glass of iced tea for summery drink.

Lavender Cupcakes

Makes 8

Put 8 paper cupcake cases in a shallow bun tin. Put 50g softened butter, 50g caster sugar and 2 teaspoons **lavender syrup** in a bowl. Beat together with a wooden spoon until just mixed. Add 1 beaten medium egg and sift over 50g self-raising flour. Beat together until light and fluffy. Divide the mixture between the cake cases, then bake at 190°C/fan 180°C/gas 3 for 12 minutes until golden (the cakes will rise about three-quarters of the way up the cases). Leave in the tin for a few minutes, then transfer to a wire rack to cool. For the icing, sift 75g icing sugar into a bowl. Gently heat 1 tablespoon lavender syrup and 10g butter in a small saucepan until melted. Pour over the icing sugar and mix well. It should be a very thick pourable consistency; if necessary, stir in a few more drops of lavender syrup. Spoon over the cakes and leave to set.

Lemon Barley Water

This delicious old-fashioned drink should be served diluted with chilled water and ice. Lemon barley water was very popular during the Victorian era when it was considered to be a healthy tonic. It can be made at any time of year, but is well known for being served during the tennis season.

Keeps for 3 weeks
Makes about 1 litre

150g pearl barley
1 litre boiling water
2 unwaxed lemons
75g caster sugar

1. Rinse the barley in a sieve under cold running water, then tip into a saucepan. Pour over the water and bring to the boil. Lower the heat, cover the lid and simmer gently for 15 minutes.
2. Meanwhile, finely grate the zest from the lemons, avoiding the white pith. Add to the pan with the sugar and stir until the sugar has dissolved. Gently simmer for a further 2–3 minutes, then turn off the heat, cover the pan and leave to cool.
3. Squeeze the juice from the lemons and add to the cooled barley water. Stir, then strain through a fine-meshed sieve into a jug.
4. Pour into a sterilized bottle with a screw-top lid and store in the fridge for up to three weeks. Serve diluted with chilled water to taste; you'll probably need about half a glass of lemon barley water topped up with chilled water. Add a few ice cubes if liked.

Variations

For lemon and ginger barley water, add a 2cm piece of fresh root ginger, peeled and thinly sliced, with the lemon zest.

For orange barley water, use 2 unwaxed oranges instead of lemons, and reduce the sugar to 50g.

Raspberry Cordial

If you grow your own raspberries and are lucky enough to have a glut, make this gloriously pink cordial. The addition of red wine vinegar brings out the flavour of the fresh fruit and adds a delicious slightly tangy note to this drink, as well as helping to preserve it.

Keeps for 2–3 months
Makes about 500ml

450g raspberries
450g caster sugar
2½ tbsp red wine vinegar
300ml water

1. Put the raspberries, sugar and vinegar in a large saucepan. Add 4 tablespoons of the water and heat gently, stirring occasionally, until the sugar has completely dissolved. Cook over a very low heat for 8–10 minutes until the mixture forms a thick pulp.
2. Spoon into a plastic or stainless-steel sieve and rub the purée through into a clean pan. Return the seeds and any pulp left in the sieve to the original pan. Add the remaining water and heat gently, then sieve again into the pan with the raspberry purée.
3. Bring the mixture to the boil and simmer for 1 minute. Turn off the heat and leave to cool for 10 minutes.
4. Pour the cooled liquid into small warm sterilized bottles and seal. The cordial will keep unopened for 2–3 months. Once opened, store in the fridge.

Cook's notes

Add a couple of teaspoons of this cordial to vinaigrette dressings to sweeten and enliven. It works well with slightly bitter leaves such as endive and frisée, and with ingredients such as avocados.

Gently stir into half-frozen home-made vanilla ice cream to make raspberry ripple, then freeze until solid.

Cheat's Berry Crème Brûlée

Serves 8

Divide 450g fresh or mixed frozen berries, such as raspberries, strawberries and blackcurrants, between eight heatproof ramekin dishes (if using frozen fruit, there's no need to defrost first). Spoon 1 tablespoon of **raspberry cordial** over each. Mix together a 250g tub of mascarpone cheese and 50g caster sugar in a large bowl. Gradually mix in a 500g carton of ready-made custard, then gently whisk for 2–3 minutes until the mixture thickens. Spoon the mixture over the fruit and smooth the surface. Chill for at least 2 hours. Sprinkle the tops generously with caster sugar, preferably golden caster sugar, and put under a hot grill for a few minutes to caramelize (watch carefully and remove as soon as the sugar is golden brown). Leave to stand for 5 minutes before serving.

Redcurrant Shrub

Shrub syrups were originally a way of preserving fruit juice in the days before home refrigeration. Non-alcoholic ones often use vinegar (see Strawberry Shrub page 86); others are made with alcohol, usually rum or brandy, as here. A shrub should have a flavour that is both tart and sweet: tangy redcurrants are perfect.

Keeps for 2 years
Makes about 1 litre

500g redcurrants
200ml water
About 600ml rum or brandy
Thinly pared rind of 1 unwaxed orange
Pinch of freshly grated nutmeg (optional)
About 300g granulated sugar

1. Wash the redcurrants (there's no need to take them off their stalks) and put in a pan with the water. Bring to the boil, lower the heat, then cover the pan and simmer for 40 minutes or until they are very soft and pulpy.
2. Tip the mixture into a suspended jelly bag (see page 6) and leave to drip-drain for several hours or overnight. Do not squeeze the pulp or the juice will be cloudy. Measure the juice: there should be about 300ml.
3. Pour the redcurrant juice into a large, clean, wide-necked jar. Add the rum or brandy, using double the quantity of alcohol to redcurrant juice (i.e., if there is 300ml juice, add 600ml alcohol). Add the orange rind and nutmeg if using. Stir the mixture together (it will thicken to a jelly-like consistency, but will become liquid again when the sugar is added later). Seal the jar and leave in a cool dark place for a week.
4. Pour the mixture into a pan and add the sugar, adding 1g sugar for every 1ml juice (i.e., for 300ml juice, add 300g

sugar). Heat gently, stirring occasionally, until the sugar has completely dissolved.

5. Strain the shrub through a muslin-lined sieve and pour into sterilized bottles. Seal and store in a cool dark place for several months before drinking to allow the syrup to mature. Use within 2 years of making.

Cook's notes

Shrub is usually served on its own and undiluted as an aperitif.

If you are using rum, choose a white or a golden rum, such as Barbados, rather than a dark, spiced rum.

Rosemary-infused Vodka

Warm and almost pine-scented, rosemary can be used to make an aromatic vodka with a distinctly Mediterranean taste. It adds a delicious twist to a Bloody Mary.

Keeps for several years
Makes about 1 litre

3 sprigs rosemary, 12–15cm in length
1 litre vodka

1. Rinse the rosemary under cold running water to remove dust if necessary, shake off excess water, then allow to air-dry.
2. Push the rosemary into a bottle or large, clean, sealable jar, such as a one-litre Kilner jar, and pour over the vodka. Seal the bottle or jar and leave in a cool dark place for two to five days.
3. Taste the vodka after the second day; the rosemary will add flavour quickly, so check it every day until the strength is to your liking.
4. Pour the infused vodka through a muslin-lined sieve into a jug, then discard the rosemary and pour the flavoured vodka into a bottle. Seal and store in a cool dark place.

Cook's notes

Make sure you use unsprayed rosemary when making this, and pick younger stems as older ones may add a slightly woody flavour.

For a classic Bloody Mary, put a slice of lemon and a few ice cubes in a tall glass. Add ½–1 teaspoon Worcestershire sauce, a pinch of celery salt, a grind of black pepper and 3–5 drops Tabasco sauce. Fill the glass to about 4cm from the top with tomato juice. Add a measure of rosemary-infused vodka and stir before serving.

Try making a rosemary vodka and tonic: pour the rosemary-infused vodka over ice and top up with tonic water. Add either a splash of fresh lemon juice or a wedge of lemon. Garnish with a small sprig of fresh rosemary, if you like.

Variation

You can also make lavender-infused vodka in the same way, although it may take a little longer for the vodka to infuse.

Rose Petal Syrup

This syrup can vary in colour from the palest pink to a deep ruby, depending on the roses used. Gather petals early in the morning from flowers that are just opening, as this is when the fragrance is strongest.

Keeps for 2 months
Makes about 600ml

250g fresh rose petals
450g caster sugar
500ml water
Freshly squeezed juice of 1 lemon

1. Taste the white base of one of the petals; this is slightly bitter in some rose varieties. If so, cut off the bases of each clump of petals.
2. Put the petals in a bowl, layering up with about half of the sugar. As you work, rub petals gently with your fingertips to bruise them a little and release the perfume. Cover the bowl with cling film and leave in a cool place for at least 6 hours or overnight.
3. Tip the petals and sugar into a pan and add the rest of the sugar and the water. Heat gently, stirring occasionally, until the sugar has completely dissolved.
4. Add the lemon juice, then continue to heat, keeping the syrup just below boiling point, for 20 minutes. Turn up the heat a little and simmer for 1 minute. Turn off the heat, cover the pan with a lid and leave to cool.
5. Strain the syrup through a fine-meshed sieve or muslin-lined colander into sterilized bottles and seal. Store in a cool dark place for up to two months. Once opened, keep in the fridge.

Cook's notes

Ideally, use the syrup within a month of making, as it will gradually lose its fragrance with time.

Make sure that you use unsprayed roses, preferably those you have grown yourself: florist and other shop-bought roses will almost definitely have been sprayed with pesticides. Smell the roses before picking. If they have little or no fragrance, neither will your syrup!

Sticky Rose Syrup Cakes

Makes 8

Made with semolina and ground almonds instead of flour, these cakes are gluten-free. Preheat the oven to 200°C/fan 190°C/gas 6 and brush eight holes in a non-stick muffin tin with a little oil. Line the base of each with a small circle of baking parchment. Cream together 85g caster sugar and 100g softened butter until creamy. Beat in 4 tablespoons of **rose petal syrup** and 100g ground almonds, then gradually add 2 medium beaten eggs. Add 100g semolina, 2 teaspoons baking powder and ½ teaspoon ground cinnamon and fold into the mixture. Spoon into the oiled muffin tin. Bake the cakes for 15 minutes. Remove from the oven, leave for 2–3 minutes, then loosen the sides with a blunt knife. Turn out onto a wire rack and remove the baking parchment. Spoon 2 teaspoons of rose syrup over the tops of each cake while still warm. Serve on small plates topped with double cream, whipped with a drizzle of rose syrup; best eaten with a fork.

Rhubarb and Rose Cordial

This rich-coloured cordial is made with summer rhubarb, which has much thicker stems and a more robust flavour than spring (forced) rhubarb and is also slightly sharper. Rose water works well with rhubarb and gives this an exotic flavour.

Keeps for 1 month
Makes about 1 litre

500g rhubarb, washed, trimmed and roughly chopped
400g granulated sugar
400ml water
2 tbsp freshly squeezed lime juice
2–3 tsp rose water

1. Put the rhubarb and sugar in a non-aluminium saucepan. Stir well and leave to stand for 30 minutes.
2. Add the water, then heat gently, stirring occasionally, until the sugar has dissolved. Bring to the boil and simmer, uncovered, for 25 minutes or until the rhubarb is mushy and the liquid slightly reduced.
3. Add the lime juice and cook for a further 2–3 minutes. Turn off the heat and leave to cool.
4. Strain the cordial through a fine stainless steel or plastic sieve, leaving the fruit to drain for about an hour, or until all the liquid has dripped through (don't squeeze it, or you will make the cordial cloudy).
5. Add the rose water, stir well, then pour the cordial into bottles. Seal and store in the fridge for up to a month. Serve diluted with chilled sparkling or soda water.

Fresh Fruit Jellies

Serves 4

Pour 150ml clear fruit juice, such as apple or white grape, into a saucepan. Add six leaves of gelatine, snipped in quarters with kitchen scissors. Leave to soak for 5 minutes. Gently heat the pan, stirring occasionally, until the gelatine has completely dissolved, but do not let it boil. Take the pan off the heat and stir in a further 350ml of fruit juice and 6 tablespoons **rhubarb and rose cordial**. Stir well and leave to cool. Meanwhile, divide 250g fresh ripe fruit, such as berries, peaches, pears or grapes, between four glasses. Pour over the jelly and leave in the fridge for 2 hours to set.

Rumtopf

Although this is really a dessert, after the rum-soaked fruit has been ladled out of the pot, the remaining rum is often served as an alcoholic cordial or after-dinner liqueur. A rumtopf is a large stoneware or ceramic pot made especially for preserving summer and autumn fruit to enjoy during the winter months. Literally meaning 'rum pot', it makes a fantastic Christmas dessert. It was first created by German seafarers who were trying to preserve fruit on their voyage from the West Indies to Germany more than 200 years ago and has been enjoyed ever since!

Keeps for several months

450g ripe strawberries, hulled
450g caster sugar
70cl bottle (700ml) dark unflavoured rum (at least 40% proof)
To add later
Raspberries
Nectarines, peaches, apricots or plums, skinned, halved and stoned
Black or green grapes, left whole
Cherries, stoned
Mango, peeled, stoned and diced
Kiwi, skinned and sliced
Pears, peeled, cored and quartered
225g caster sugar for every 450g fruit

1. Put the strawberries in a large bowl, sprinkling sugar between each layer. Leave for 1 hour, then carefully tip into the rumtopf. If you don't have a rumtopf, use a ceramic container with a loose-fitting lid; if you use clear glass, store in a dark place or the fruit will discolour. Cover with rum to a depth of about 1cm.
2. Cover the surface of the fruit with cling film then top with a light saucer or side plate to keep the fruit submerged. Cover the pot with cling film, put on the lid and leave in a cool dark place.
3. Continue adding layers of fruit to the rumtopf as they come into season, mixing them with sugar and covering with rum

each time. When you have finished, store in a cool place for at least one month and up to three months, to mature.

Cook's notes

Serve the fruit and some of the syrup as a dessert on its own or with whipped cream. It's also good in trifles and as a pancake filling. The remaining syrup can be strained, bottled and served as a liqueur.

All fruit should be in perfect condition; just ripe but still firm and clean. If you need to wash fruit such as strawberries or grapes, let them dry on kitchen paper before using.

Many fruits can be added to a rumtopf, but those with a high water content such as melon should be avoided. Apples, bananas, blackberries, blueberries, gooseberries and rhubarb should also be left out.

Scented Geranium Syrup

Scented geraniums are fragrant-leaved perennials of the pelargonium family and were widely grown in the Victorian era for perfumery, potpourris and culinary purposes. The scent of the leaves varies from citrus and rose to mint, nuts, spices and chocolate and is often indicated by the name of the variety: 'Attar of roses', 'Lemon fancy', 'Orange fizz', 'Hansen's wild spice' and 'Peppermint lace' are just a few examples.

Keeps for 4 months
Makes about 300ml

6 large scented geranium leaves or 12 small ones (see Cook's notes)
300g caster sugar
300ml water

1. Rinse the leaves under cold running water to remove any dirt or dust, then leave to dry on kitchen paper. Roughly chop the leaves.
2. Put the sugar and water into a saucepan. Heat gently, stirring occasionally, until the sugar has completely dissolved.
3. Add the geranium leaves to the syrup and bring to the boil. Simmer for 2 minutes, then turn off the heat, cover the pan with a lid and leave the syrup to cool.
4. Strain the syrup through a sieve into a jug and pour into sterilized bottles. Store in a cool dry place for up to four months.

Cook's notes

Make sure you use scented geranium leaves for this syrup and not those from ordinary garden geraniums. Some varieties are more suited for syrup-making than others; rose and lemon-scented geraniums usually have the most intense fragrance. Pick a small leaf and crush it between your fingers. If it is very fragrant and you love the scent, it will make a good syrup. Use for flavouring cakes, jellies, sweet sauces and jams.

Scented Geranium Sponge

Grease a 900g loaf tin and line with baking parchment. Sift 225g self-raising flour and 1 teaspoon baking powder into a bowl. Add 175g softened unsalted butter, 175g caster sugar, 3 beaten eggs and 1 tablespoon **scented geranium syrup** and beat well until the mixture is smooth and creamy. Pour and scrape the mixture into the prepared tin and level the surface. Bake at 180°C/fan 170°C/gas 4 for 30 minutes, then turn down the oven to 170°C/fan 160°C/gas 3. Bake for a further 20 minutes until well risen and firm and a skewer inserted into the middle comes out clean. Leave to cool in the tin for 30 minutes, then remove the cake and place on a cooling rack. When completely cold, make the icing: Sift 150g icing sugar into a bowl. Add 5 teaspoons scented geranium syrup and mix until smooth. The icing should thickly coat the back of a spoon; add a further teaspoon of syrup if it is too stiff. Spread the icing evenly over the cake and leave to set. You can decorate it depending of the flavour of the syrup, for example with lemon zest or rose petals.

Strawberry Liqueur (Crème de Fraises)

This is a stunningly deep red colour and would make a lovely Valentine's Day gift. Be sure to use flavoursome, fully ripe but unblemished strawberries, freshly picked if possible.

Keeps for 1 year
Makes about 750ml

350g ripe strawberries
300g caster sugar
450ml vodka (unflavoured) or gin
2 tsp lemon juice
200ml water

1. Wash the strawberries if necessary and allow to dry on a tray spread with kitchen paper. Remove the green hulls, then cut each strawberry in half.
2. Put the strawberries in a large, clean, sealable jar, such as a one-litre Kilner jar, sprinkling 100g of the sugar between the strawberries (this will start to draw out the juice). Pour over the vodka or gin, close the jar and store in a cool dark place for two to three days.
3. Check the jar daily and give it a gentle shake to dissolve the sugar. The vodka is ready when it is a very deep red colour.
4. Put the remaining 200g of sugar, the lemon juice and water in a saucepan. Bring to the boil, stirring frequently until the sugar has completely dissolved. Lower the heat and simmer for 2–3 minutes, then turn off the heat and leave to cool.
5. Strain the strawberry-infused alcohol through a fine-meshed sieve or muslin-lined colander into a bowl. Pour into a jug, then decant into sterilized bottles and seal.
6. Store in a cool dark place and let the strawberry liqueur mature for at least a month before drinking; it will improve

with age. Use within a year of making and once opened, store in the fridge and drink within two months.

Cook's note

Strawberry liqueur (crème de fraises) is a lovely accompaniment to fresh fruit desserts and is particularly good in champagne and sparkling wine drinks and cocktails.

Strawberry Shrub

This old-fashioned syrup dates back to the eighteenth century where adding vinegar to the fruit helped to prevent it from spoiling in the hot weather. The vinegar balances the sweetness of the sugar, making this a refreshing summer drink. The word 'shrub' comes from the Arabic *sharab*, which means 'to drink'.

Keeps for 6 months
Makes about 450ml

450g ripe strawberries
300–400ml cider vinegar
400g caster sugar

1. Wash and hull the strawberries, then cut into thick slices and pack tightly in a bowl, leaving as few gaps as possible. Pour over just enough of the vinegar to cover. Cover the bowl with cling film and leave in the fridge for three to four days.
2. Remove from the fridge and strain the vinegar, discarding the strawberries. Pour the vinegar into a pan and add the sugar. Gently heat, stirring occasionally, until the sugar has completely dissolved.
3. Bring to the boil and simmer for 2–3 minutes. Turn off the heat and leave to cool. Pour into sterilized bottles, seal and store in a cool dark place. Use within six months of making. Serve the shrub with chilled water, diluting 1 part shrub to 4 parts water.

Cook's notes

This is an ideal way to use up less-than-perfect strawberries, but make sure you remove any parts that are brown or mushy.

Use raspberry vinegar rather than cider vinegar for a really intense fruity flavour and colour.

Use a spoonful or two of this when making a salad dressing to add a touch of sweetness.

Autumn

Make the most of the remaining warm weather. As the first of the leaves begin to fall, the hedgerow harvest begins in earnest. Blackberries are easy to find in abundance and are around for at least a month, although once picked they don't keep well, so make sure you have all other ingredients and equipment ready for use. Alternatively, you can pop them in the freezer and make cordials and syrups on wet-weather days; blackberries' natural high sugar content makes fabulous rich-coloured cordials and liqueurs such as Bramble Cordial, Blackberry Shrub and Crème de Mure. They have great affinity with apples, so try a mixture of the two for a really fruity flavour. Other fruit and berries, such as rosehips, elderberries and sloes can also be gathered for free; Sloe Gin is an absolute must, if you haven't made it before. Succulent ripe plums and damsons and less well-known fruits such as quinces and medlars can be found at this time of year and are delicious made into Damson and Cinnamon or Medlar Syrup, and Quince Ratafia.

Blackberry Shrub

This is a variation on the traditional shrub made with vinegar, but here citric acid provides the sharp flavour. This is a natural preservative and can be bought from wine-making and brewing shops, chemists and online. You can use all blackberries for this cordial or a combination of other berries – frozen ones are fine – such as strawberries, raspberries and redcurrants.

Keeps for 3 weeks
Makes about 600ml

1.5kg fresh or frozen blackberries (or a combination of blackberries and other berries)
4 tbsp water
About 350g granulated sugar
About 1 tsp citric acid

1. Check that the berries are clean, hull them if necessary (strawberries) or remove from the stalks (redcurrants) and put in a large saucepan.
2. Add the water and heat gently until the fruit juice runs freely. Bring to the boil and boil for 2 minutes, gently crushing the fruit with a potato masher to extract the juice. Don't be too heavy-handed when crushing blackberries as crushed pips may make the shrub slightly bitter.
3. Cover and leave to cool for 10 minutes, then strain the fruit through a muslin-lined sieve or jelly bag. Gently squeeze the fruit left in the muslin or bag (the shrub will be slightly cloudy).
4. Measure the juice and pour back into the cleaned pan. Add 175g of sugar for every 300ml of juice. Gently heat, stirring frequently until the sugar has completely dissolved. Turn off the heat, then stir in ½ teaspoon of citric acid for every 300ml of juice that was measured.

5. Pour the shrub into sterilized bottles and store in the fridge for up to three weeks, or preserve the syrup using the water-bath method (see page 10), seal and store in a cool dark place for up to a year. Once opened, keep the shrub in the fridge and use within three weeks.

Cook's note
Serve the shrub diluted with hot or cold water to taste or with chilled dry white wine instead of water.

Blackberry Whisky

This has a gorgeous deep, dark purple colour and a lovely fruity flavour. The blackberries are removed after three months and the whisky can be enjoyed straight away; it's a great drink to serve at Christmas. Leaving it for a few months will help the flavour to mature and mellow further.

Keeps for 2 years
Makes about 750ml

1kg clean dry blackberries
250g caster or granulated sugar
70cl bottle (700ml) whisky

1. Put the blackberries in a large, clean, sealable jar, one layer at a time sprinkling the sugar between the layers. Add the whisky, then close the jar and give it a gentle shake.
2. Store in a cool dark place for a week, giving the jar a daily shake, until all the sugar has dissolved. Leave the jar for a further three months undisturbed.
3. Strain the whisky through a muslin-lined sieve into a large jug and pour into sterilized bottles. You can drink the whisky straight away, but the flavour improves as it matures. Drink within 2 years of making.

Cook's notes

Use a good-quality whisky for this, but not expensive single malt.

Pick blackberries on a warm sunny day if possible, choosing only the best berries: over-ripe and under-ripe ones will spoil the flavour.

The whisky-infused berries can be used for a dessert. Try pushing them through a fine sieve to make a delicious whisky-flavoured blackberry purée that's perfect for serving with ice cream.

Blackberry Hot Toddy

Serves 2

This warming drink soothes even the most miserable cold. Put 4 slices of fresh root ginger and 1 teaspoon clear honey in a pan with 150ml water. Slowly bring to the boil and simmer for 1 minute. Turn off the heat and leave to infuse for 5 minutes. Add 150ml **blackberry whisky** and stir well. Strain into heatproof glasses and sip slowly.

Bramble Cordial

Blackberries are at their best between late August and mid-September, although you may still be able to pick them as late as October. They do not keep well – not even for a day – but if you don't have time to use them immediately after picking, frozen berries will work well in this simple deep-purple coloured cordial.

Keeps for 6 weeks
Makes about 300ml

450g ripe blackberries
100g caster sugar
6 tbsp water
1 tbsp freshly squeezed lemon juice

1. Put the blackberries in a bowl and cover with cold water. Skim off any dust or bits that float the surface, then drain immediately (do not soak the blackberries for more than a minute) and put in a saucepan.
2. Add the sugar to the blackberries, stir briefly, then cover the pan and leave for 30 minutes.
3. Add 4 tablespoons of the water and the lemon juice. Slowly bring to the boil, stirring occasionally to dissolve the sugar. Bring to the boil and simmer for 5 minutes.
4. Gently crush the blackberries with a potato masher to release the juices (do not press too hard or the cordial may be bitter).
5. Pour the pulp into a jelly bag or muslin-lined sieve or colander and leave to drain over a bowl. When the juices have stopped dripping, stir the final 2 tablespoons of water into the blackberry pulp and gently squeeze out the remaining juice by pressing down with the back of metal spoon.
6. Pour the cordial into sterilized bottles and seal. Store in the fridge for up to six weeks.

> **Cook's note**
>
> Stir a few spoonfuls of blackcurrant cordial into chopped or sliced apples or pears when making a pie or crumble; it adds both flavour and an attractive pinkish-purple colour to the fruit.

Autumn Fruit Pudding

Serves 6

Put 450g peeled, cored and roughly chopped eating apples in a pan with 450g halved, stoned and roughly chopped ripe plums. Add 100ml **bramble cordial** and 100g caster sugar. Bring to the boil, stirring occasionally to dissolve the sugar, then gently simmer for 15 minutes or until the apple pieces are soft and the liquid thick and syrupy. Turn off the heat and leave to cool. Line the inside of a 1.5 litre pudding basin with day-old white bread; you will need about 10 slices. First cut a round of bread to fit the bottom of the basin, then cut the remaining bread into wide lengths and arrange all but a few around the sides of the basin, overlapping them. Reserve 6 tablespoons of the juices from the fruit, then spoon the rest of the cooled fruit into the bread-lined basin, filling almost to the top. Cover with the remaining slices of bread. Put a plate on top of the pudding and weigh it down with a tin of beans or tomatoes etc. from your store cupboard. Chill in the fridge overnight. To serve, run a knife around the edge of the pudding and turn out onto a serving plate. Brush or drizzle the reserved juices over the outside.

Crab Apple Cordial

Crab apples may not be particularly attractive; the small, misshapen, spotty fruit seem to be little more than skin and pips and are also mouth-puckeringly sour when eaten raw. However, when cooked, they make the most superb jelly and deep pink cordial with an intensely sweet but slightly sharp flavour.

Keeps for 3 months
Makes about 1 litre

1kg crab apples
700ml water
About 350g granulated sugar
Juice of 1 small lemon

1. Wash and roughly chop the crab apples. Put them in a large saucepan with 600ml of the water and slowly bring to the boil. Simmer gently for 30 minutes or until the apples are very soft and pulpy.
2. Pour the pulp into a jelly bag or muslin-lined sieve and leave to drip overnight into a large bowl. Do not squeeze the pulp or the cordial will be cloudy.
3. Measure the juice and return to the cleaned pan. For every 100ml of juice add 70g sugar. Add the lemon juice and the remaining 100ml of water.
4. Gently heat, stirring occasionally, until the sugar has dissolved. Bring to the boil, then turn off the heat. Skim off any white froth from the surface, then pour into warm, sterilized bottles and seal. Use within three months of making. Once opened, store in the fridge.

Cook's notes

Don't forget to add the extra water when dissolving the sugar, as otherwise the high amount of pectin in the apples may turn the cordial into jelly in the bottles.

Add a few spoonfuls of this cordial when cooking apples for desserts and sauces for rich meats, such as pork or game.

Crème de Mure

There's an abundance of blackberries in hedgerows and woodlands during the warm months of early autumn and, best of all, they are completely free. Crème de mure – blackberry liqueur – is an excellent alternative to the more well-known crème de cassis for those who do not grow their own blackcurrants.

Keeps for 4 months
Makes about 1 litre

500g blackberries
70cl bottle (700ml) red wine (see Cook's notes)
350g granulated sugar
250ml brandy

1. Discard any bruised or damaged blackberries, then put in a bowl of cold water. Skim off any dust and bits that rise to the top of the water and drain.
2. Put the blackberries in a large saucepan and gently crush with a potato masher. Pour over the red wine, stir, then cover and leave for 48 hours.
3. Strain through a muslin-lined sieve, squeezing out as much juice as possible, then return the juice to the washed pan.
4. Add the sugar and gently heat, stirring occasionally, until the sugar has dissolved. Keep the liquid just below simmering point for about an hour, to reduce and slightly thicken the syrup. Turn off the heat and leave to cool.
5. Stir in the brandy, pour into sterilized bottles and seal. Drink within four months of making.

Cook's notes

Blackberry juices can stain, so take care when making this liqueur or wear old clothes!

Buy a good fruity red wine for making this, one that you would enjoy drinking on its own. A very cheap wine will spoil the flavour.

This makes an excellent sauce for serving with duck or game: simply simmer until well-reduced, then season with salt and pepper.

Unflavoured vodka can be used instead of brandy, if preferred.

Little Red Riding Hood

Serves 1

This demure-sounding cocktail is very fruity with a definite 'bite'. It also contains Crème de Fraises (page 84). Put 1 measure/1½ tablespoons gin, ¾ measure/1 tablespoon **crème de mure**, ¾ measure/1 tablespoon crème de fraises, and 1½ measures/2 tablespoons orange juice in a cocktail shaker with ice. Shake well, then strain into a cocktail glass half-filled with crushed ice. Decorate with fresh fruit.

Damson and Cinnamon Syrup

This syrup can be made with any plums – cultivated or wild – but is especially good with smaller hedgerow plums such as damsons and bullaces because they tend to have a stronger flavour and more acidity. There's no need to remove the fiddly stones as they will be strained out of the syrup later.

Keeps for 4 months
Makes about 750ml

600g ripe plums
450g caster or granulated sugar
1 cinnamon stick
Juice of 1 lemon
400ml water

1. Roughly cut each plum into two or three pieces; the easiest way is to slice off the ends either side of the stone, leaving the chunk in the middle with the stone.
2. Put the chopped plums in a large saucepan with the sugar and cinnamon stick and mix together. Pour over the lemon juice, then cover the pan with a lid and leave for 1 hour.
3. Pour over the water, then gently heat, stirring occasionally, until the sugar has dissolved. Bring to a very gentle simmer – the mixture should barely bubble – and cook uncovered for 25–30 minutes or until the fruit is very soft and pulpy. Turn off the heat, cover the pan with a lid and leave to cool for about 20 minutes.
4. Strain the syrup through a fine-meshed sieve or muslin-lined colander into a bowl, then pour through a funnel into sterilized bottles. Seal and store for up to four months.

Cook's note

Plums come in a wide range of sizes, colours and sweetness; try eating one before making this syrup. If it is very sweet you may like to reduce the sugar (but not too much or it won't keep well); if it is very sharp, add just a little more sugar and leave out the lemon juice.

Eve's Pudding

Serves 4

Peel, core and chop 400g eating apples. Put in a bowl and pour over 4 tablespoons **damson and cinnamon syrup.** Mix well to coat the apples and transfer to a buttered, ovenproof baking dish. Put 50g softened butter, 50g soft light brown sugar, 50g self-raising flour and 1 beaten egg in a bowl and beat together. Add 1 tablespoon milk and beat again until smooth and light. Spoon and spread over the apples. Bake at 180°C/fan 170°C/gas 4 for 40 minutes or until the sponge is dark golden and springs back when gently pushed with a finger. Leave to settle and cool for a few minutes. Serve with pouring cream or thick custard.

Elderberry Cordial

The wild elder is one of the most prolific providers of ingredients for syrups and cordials. Earlier in the year they are covered in perfumed creamy-coloured blossoms, then at the end of summer and throughout autumn, heavy clusters of purple-black fruits can be found,

Keeps for 3 weeks
Makes about 2 litres

750g elderberries
2 litres water
225g caster sugar

1. Use a fork to remove the berries from their stalks. Wash in cold water, then drain in a colander.
2. Put the berries in a large saucepan with the water and slowly bring to the boil. Gently simmer, uncovered, for about 15 minutes or until the fruit is very soft and pulpy. Turn off the heat and leave to stand for 15 minutes.
3. Pour the elderberries and liquid through a jelly bag or a nylon or stainless-steel sieve lined with muslin, placed over a large bowl. Leave to drip for 2 hours to extract as much juice as possible but do not squeeze or the cordial will be cloudy.
4. Return the liquid to the cleaned pan and add the sugar. Gently heat until the sugar has dissolved, then leave to cool. Decant into sterilized bottles, seal and store in the fridge for up to three weeks, or freeze in small plastic bottles.

Cook's note

When collecting elderberries, never strip a tree bare; try to pick from several trees instead.

Pear and Elderberry Sorbet

Serves 6

Peel, core and chop 1kg ripe pears. Put in a pan with 150ml **elderberry cordial** and 1 bay leaf. Bring to the boil, lower the heat, cover the pan and gently simmer for 15 minutes or until the pears are very tender. Leave to cool. Meanwhile, put 100g caster sugar in heavy-based pan with 150ml water. Slowly bring to the boil, stirring occasionally, until the sugar has completely dissolved, then simmer uncovered for 5 minutes. Remove the pan from the heat and leave to cool. Remove the bay leaf from the pears and purée the fruit in a blender or food processor. Add the syrup and 1 tablespoon lemon juice and blend for a few more seconds to mix. Chill in the fridge for 2 hours.

Churn in an ice cream maker according to the manufacturer's instructions, then serve immediately or transfer to a freezer container. Alternatively, pour into a freezer container and freeze for 1½ hours or until the sides and base are just frozen. Remove from the freezer and beat to break up the ice crystals, then quickly return to the freezer. Repeat this process two more times and then freeze until solid. Remove from the freezer 10 minutes before serving to allow the sorbet to soften slightly.

Hawthorn and Rosehip Cordial

Hawthorn berries are plentiful but can be challenging to pick as the branches are prickly. Their flavour is similar to very ripe apples and the berries, although very attractive, are mostly pips, so you do need to pick a lot when making syrup. They work really well combined with rosehips as here and with warm, fragrant spices.

Keeps for 3 months
Makes about 1.5 litres

500g hawthorn berries
500g rosehips
1.5 litres water
½ tsp ground cinnamon
4 whole cloves
100g soft light brown sugar
100g caster sugar

1. Wash the two types of berries separately. Gently squeeze most of the pips out of the hawthorn berries and discard. Roughly chop the rosehips.
2. Put both types of berries in a large pan with 1 litre of the water. Add the cinnamon and cloves and slowly bring to the boil. Gently simmer for 5 minutes, then remove from the heat, cover with a lid and leave to steep for 30 minutes.
3. Remove the spices, then use a potato masher to crush the berries to a pulp. Tip the mixture into a fine-meshed sieve set over a large bowl.
4. When the liquid has drained, tip the pulp back into the pan. Add the remaining 500ml water, bring to the boil and simmer for a further 5 minutes. Again, tip the mixture into the sieve over a separate bowl and leave to drain.

5. Pour both lots of liquid back into the cleaned pan and add the sugar. Slowly bring to the bowl, stirring until the sugar has dissolved. Bring to the boil and simmer for 2 minutes. Turn off the heat and leave to cool.

6. Pour the cordial through a muslin-lined sieve or colander into a large jug, then pour into sterilized bottles and seal. Store in the fridge for up to three months. Once opened, use within two weeks.

Cook's notes

Serve the cordial diluted to taste with chilled still or sparkling water. It is also good topped up with near-boiling water to make a warming drink on a cold day.

It's essential to strain the cordial through muslin as rosehips contain very fine hairs which can be an irritant.

Note: Hawthorn berries are reputedly a 'heart tonic'. Some herbalists advise against consuming drinks made from them if you are taking medication such as beta blockers, digoxin or antihistamines and suggest that they should not be consumed in large quantities by young children or pregnant women.

Medlar Syrup

Widely grown until Victorian times, medlars have a wonderful flavour when cooked, tasting like a cross between apples and dates with a lovely hint of caramel and custard. They are, however, an unattractive fruit, somewhat like small brown misshapen apples, and in medieval times were called 'dog's arse fruit', due to their appearance. They are worth seeking out and if you don't have a tree of your own, can often be found at farmers' markets in late autumn. This thick syrup is a rich, dark amber colour.

Keeps for up to 8 weeks
Makes about 600ml

1.5kg medlars, bletted (see Cook's notes)
600ml water
400g granulated sugar
2 tsp lemon juice

1. Roughly chop the fruit including the cores. Put in a large saucepan with 400ml of the water and bring to the boil. Lower the heat, cover with a lid and simmer for 30 minutes. Leave to cool for 10 minutes, then gently squash with a potato masher (don't press too hard or the syrup will be cloudy).
2. Strain the juice through a sieve or colander and set aside, then return the fruit pulp to the pan with the remaining 200ml of water. Bring back to the boil and simmer for 5 minutes.
3. Pour the first batch of juice through a muslin-lined sieve or jelly bag suspended over a large bowl, then add the second batch of fruit pulp and juice and leave it to drip for several hours to extract as much juice as possible.
4. Return the juice to the cleaned out pan and add the sugar and lemon juice. Slowly bring to the boil, stirring occasionally, until the sugar has dissolved, then gently simmer uncovered for 15 minutes to reduce and thicken the syrup.
5. Allow the syrup to cool in the pan, then ladle into sterilized jars. Seal and store in the fridge, where it keeps well for up to eight weeks.

Cook's notes

Medlars should be 'bletted' before cooking as they have very little flavour or juice until they reach this late stage of ripening. This means leaving them to mature beyond ripening point until they are deep brown, soft and slightly squashy – in other words, starting to decay. This used to be done by leaving the fruit on the tree until the first frost, but they are now usually picked while still rock-hard. The traditional method is to bury them in sawdust, but you can simply leave them in a shallow bowl at cool room temperature for about four weeks until the fruit is ready (put them in the freezer for a few hours if you want to speed up the process). Bletting also reduces the amount of pectin in the medlars.

The syrup is better stored in jars than in bottles in case the remaining pectin makes it thicken to a light set impossible to pour from a bottle. It can be used instead of golden syrup or honey in most recipes.

Medlar and Banana Teabread

Makes a 900g loaf

Lightly grease and line the base of a 900g loaf tin with baking parchment. Sift 225g self-raising flour into a bowl and add ¼ teaspoon freshly grated nutmeg. Add 100g butter or baking margarine, cut into cubes, and rub in the fat using your fingers and thumbs until the mixture resembles fine breadcrumbs. Peel and mash 1 large very ripe banana and mix with 2 beaten medium eggs, 100g soft light brown sugar and 6 tablespoons **medlar syrup**. Add to the dry ingredients, mix together then turn into the prepared tin. Bake at 180°C/fan 170°C/gas 4 for about 50 minutes or until a fine skewer inserted into the centre comes out clean. Allow the teabread to cool for 15 minutes in the tin, then turn out on to a wire rack. Brush the top with 2 tablespoons of **medlar syrup** and leave to cool. Serve thickly sliced.

Pear and Star Anise Liqueur

This is a deliciously fruity liqueur, subtly spiced with star anise. It is a little less alcoholic than some liqueurs as it contains a base of sugar syrup. You will need a little patience as it takes a few months for the liqueur to mature.

Keeps for 2 years
Makes about 1 litre

400g granulated sugar
2 whole star anise
450ml water
4 very ripe pears, peeled and sliced
Strip of rind from an unwaxed lemon
About 500ml vodka (unflavoured) or brandy

1. Put the sugar and star anise in a large saucepan and add the water. Gently heat, stirring occasionally, until the sugar has dissolved, then bring to the boil and simmer for 1 minute.
2. Turn off the heat, cover the pan with a lid and leave to cool. Remove the star anise and discard.
3. Put the pears and lemon rind in a large sterilized jar. Add the syrup, then pour in at least 450ml of vodka or brandy and a bit more if there is space in the jar. Close the jar.
4. Leave in a cool dark place for four weeks, shaking the jar every couple of days.
5. Strain the liqueur into a sterilized bottle, seal and store for three to four months before drinking to allow it to mature.

Cook's notes

The pears can be served as a dessert with whipped cream or custard.

After a few months, sediment may develop at the base of the liqueur bottle; either pour carefully, or if giving as a gift, decant into another sterilized bottle first.

Variation

Instead of star anise, you could add a couple of slices of fresh ginger, a cinnamon stick or a vanilla pod when making the sugar syrup.

Red Grape Juice

If you grow your own grapes or are given some from someone who does, this is a simple way of extracting the juice and making a sugar-free drink. It doesn't keep for long (and doesn't freeze well, either), so ideally you should serve on the same day it is made.

Keeps for 2 days
Makes about 750ml

1kg ripe and sweet red or black grapes
150ml water

1. Rinse the bunches of grapes in cold water to remove any dust and shake off the excess water. Remove the grapes from the stalks, discarding any that are green or unripe, hard, shrivelled or mouldy.
2. Put the grapes in a large saucepan and gently crush with a potato masher; you need to crush each grape and squeeze out the juice, but don't overdo it or you will release too much of the slightly bitter tannins from the skins.
3. Add the water and slowly bring to the boil. Simmer for 8-10 minutes, stirring occasionally. Turn off the heat and leave to stand for 10 minutes.
4. Strain through a fine-meshed sieve or colander into a large jug and leave until cool. Chill in the fridge before serving, diluting to taste with a little extra still or sparkling water, if liked.

Cook's notes

If possible, make the juice with freshly picked grapes: ideally harvest them mid-morning on a warm sunny day.

Taste the grape juice after simmering and add a little sugar or clear honey if you want to sweeten it a little, stirring until dissolved.

Rosehip Syrup

During and after the Second World War, when food was rationed, rosehip syrup was given to nearly every child (usually along with a less enjoyable daily dose of cod-liver oil) to supplement a diet that was often lacking in fresh fruit and vegetables. It is richer in vitamin C than many citrus fruits.

Keeps for 2 months
Makes about 1.5 litres

1kg rosehips
1 litre cold water
400ml near-boiling water
Juice of 1 lemon
400g caster or granulated sugar

1. Wash the rosehips and finely chop in a food processor. Do this in several batches, adding just enough of the cold water to each batch, so that they are chopped effectively and don't get stuck in the blades.
2. Tip the minced rosehips into a large pan and add the remainder of the cold water. Bring to the boil and simmer gently for 3–4 minutes or until the hips are very soft. Turn off the heat, cover the pan with a lid and leave to stand for 15 minutes.
3. Pour the mixture through a sieve over a large bowl and set aside. Tip the rosehip pulp back into the pan, add the near-boiling water and lemon juice and bring back to the boil. Simmer for 2–3 minutes, then turn off the heat and leave to stand for 10 minutes.
4. Pour the first batch of rosehip juice through a jelly bag or muslin-lined sieve over a large bowl. When all the juice is in the bowl, do the same with the rosehip pulp and juice in the pan. Leave it to drip through for at least an hour, but do not squeeze.
5. Tip the juice back into the cleaned out pan and bring to the boil. Simmer for 10 minutes, to reduce and thicken slightly.

6. Add the sugar and stir until dissolved. Simmer for a further 5 minutes. Turn off the heat and leave to cool for 10 minutes, then pour into warm, sterilized bottles and seal.

Cook's notes

Hips are the fruit of both the dog rose and field rose. They can be gathered from August until November, although this can be quite tricky as the bushes are thorny, so you will need to wear gloves. Don't eat the hips raw, as the inside is full of 'hairs' that can be an irritant.

The syrup is an attractive deep peach colour and is naturally cloudy. Serve diluted with cold or hot water (it's soothing when slowly sipped when you have a cold). It's really good drizzled over creamy puddings such as rice pudding and makes excellent ice lollies; dilute by up to half with water before freezing.

Sloe Cordial

Sloes are tiny, dusky purple-black, wild plums, which grow on blackthorn trees. They ripen around October and the longer you can leave the berries on the tree the better, but don't leave it too long or other people may get there first. Eaten raw, sloes are mouth-numbingly astringent, but when cooked, they make a rich, plum-flavoured cordial.

Keeps for 2 months
Makes about 750ml

1kg sloes
500ml water
1 tbsp lemon juice
About 500g caster or granulated sugar

1. Wash the sloes and put them in a large saucepan with the water. Bring to the boil, then lower the heat, cover the pan with a lid and simmer for 15 minutes, or until the sloes are very soft and pulpy. Stir in the lemon juice.
2. Tip the mixture into a jelly bag or a large sieve or colander lined with muslin. Leave to drip into a large bowl for about 3 hours or overnight. Do not press the fruit or squeeze the jelly bag.
3. Measure the juice and pour back into the cleaned pan. For every 100ml of juice, add 75g sugar. Gently heat, stirring frequently, until the sugar has dissolved, then bring to the boil. Turn off the heat and leave to cool for 10 minutes.
4. Skim off any scum that has risen to the top, then pour through a funnel into warm sterilized bottles and seal. Keep in the fridge and use within two months. Alternatively, pour into plastic bottles and freeze. To keep the cordial for up to a year, follow the water-bath sterilization method (see page 10).
5. Serve diluted with cold water or add to chilled dry sparkling wine for a celebratory drink.

Cook's notes

Take care when picking sloes as the trees and bushes have long spiky thorns; ideally wear gloves, and a hat to protect your head from low prickly branches.

If you don't have enough sloes you can make up the weight in fruit with chopped cored apples. Reduce the sugar slightly as the apples will need less sweetening.

Sloe Gin

This is probably the best known hedgerow liqueur, a gorgeous blend of juniper and almond flavour. In recent years it has become very trendy and you can even buy special 'sloe-gin bottles' in which to present your liqueur. Traditionally the sloes should be picked after they have been lightly frosted, which softens the fruit and makes them juicier. If the first frosts are late or you just can't wait, a quick blast in the freezer works just as well. Never pick the sloe branches completely bare; always leave a few berries for wildlife to enjoy and to ensure future generations of trees.

Keeps for several years
Makes about 700ml

450g sloes
450g caster or granulated sugar
70cl bottle (700ml) gin

1. Remove any bruised or damaged sloes. If you have picked them before they have been frosted, put them on a tray in the freezer for a few hours, then remove and gently crush each sloe with the back of a spoon to split the skin (don't mash them!), or you can prick each with a small skewer if you prefer.
2. Divide the sloes between two clean, medium-sized bottles or Kilner jars, then divide the sugar between them, followed by the gin. Close the containers and give them a good shake to mix and start the sugar dissolving.
3. Store in a cool, dark place and shake them daily for a week, then once a week for the next eight weeks. Taste the gin and if it has a distinctive flavour of sloes it is ready to bottle; if not, or if you prefer a stronger flavour, leave for another two weeks.
4. Strain the flavoured gin through a fine-meshed or muslin-lined sieve or a muslin-lined colander, then pour through a funnel into sterilized bottles. The sloe gin is ready to drink straight away but will improve considerably with age and unopened bottles should keep for several years.

Cook's notes

It isn't essential to freeze the sloes; some sloe gin makers prefer to use fresh firm sloes and prick each several times with a skewer or darning needle.

Sloe juice will stain your fingers and your clothes. You may wish to wear thin plastic gloves and old clothes when making this drink.

As sloe gin matures, the flavour will mellow and the colour will gradually change from ruby to tawny. It's a classic Christmas drink, so ideally make it in the autumn for Christmas the following year. Sloe gin is usually served neat in small liqueur glasses at room temperature or you can add a teaspoon or two to a glass of sparkling wine.

Variation

For sloe vodka, use a bottle of unflavoured vodka instead of gin.

Sloe Gin Cocktails

Sloe Gin and Tonic – mix two parts ordinary gin with one part **sloe gin** and top up with tonic water, ice and a slice of lemon or lime.

Charlie Chaplin (from the 1920s) – shake together with ice 2 tablespoons **sloe gin**, 2 teaspoons apricot brandy and 2 teaspoons lime juice. Strain or serve with the ice if preferred.

Sloe Gin Fizz – mix 3–4 tablespoons **sloe gin** and 1 teaspoon lemon juice together. Add crushed ice or a couple of ice cubes, then top up the glass with cream soda.

Quince Ratafia

A ratafia is an old-fashioned, fruit-infused alcoholic cordial often with almondy flavours (usually achieved by adding the kernels or pips of the fruit). It was reputedly Jane Austen's favourite drink. Quinces are a lovely aromatic fruit and are perfect for this liqueur.

Keeps for 2 years
Makes about 500ml

2 large or 3 medium ripe quinces
250g caster sugar
2 strips of rind from an unwaxed lemon
½ cinnamon stick
2 whole cloves
500ml brandy
1 tsp almond extract (optional)

1. Wash and carefully dry the quinces on kitchen paper, then grate the whole fruit, including the skins and cores. The grated flesh will brown quickly, so as soon as you have grated one, layer it up in a large, clean, sealable jar, such as a one-litre Kilner jar, with some of the sugar, lemon rind, cinnamon and cloves and cover with a splash of the brandy.
2. Grate the remaining quince(s) and layer in the same way, then sprinkle over any remaining sugar and pour over the rest of the brandy.
3. Close the jar and leave in a cool dark place for a week, gently shaking the jar daily to dissolve the sugar. Leave for a further three months undisturbed.
4. Strain the quince-flavoured brandy through a fine-meshed sieve or muslin-lined colander, stir in the almond extract if using, then pour into sterilized bottles. You can drink the ratafia straight away, but the flavour improves as it matures. Drink within 2 years of making.

Cook's notes

Quinces are usually picked while still green and unripe. Let them ripen to yellow before using; you'll know when they are ready as they have a strong fragrance when at their peak. Handle carefully as they bruise easily.

Variation

Although ratafia is usually made with brandy, you can make quince vodka in exactly the same way, substituting unflavoured vodka for the brandy.

Winter

When it comes to fresh fruit, flowers and herbs, winter is the bleakest month; there is little growing in the garden or in the wild that can be used for drink-making. Hopefully you will still be enjoying cordials and syrups made earlier in the year, but before you think about settling into your fireside chair, there are still plenty of drinks you can make.

This is a great season for making liqueurs such as Amaretto, Coffee Liqueur and Crème de Cacao. With Christmas just round the corner, you'll find recipes here for Egg Nog and Mulling Syrup for making mulled wine, both perfect for welcoming guests. If you are looking for an after-dinner tipple, try Chocolate or Irish Cream Liqueur.

Not every recipe here contains alcohol and there are still plenty of soft drinks to make including Pomegranate and Clementine and Cinnamon cordials. You can also make fresh fruit beverages from frozen summer fruits and Cherry Berry Cordial should give you a good boost of vitamin C to ward off winter sniffles.

Amaretto

Commercially, amaretto is made by steeping crushed almond and apricot kernels in alcohol. This version is much simpler and produces surprisingly similar results. Use natural almond and vanilla extract (but without the little black seeds) rather than cheap essence for a smooth-tasting liqueur. Little amaretti biscuits are a classic accompaniment.

Keeps for 1 year
Makes about 600ml

100g demerara sugar
200g caster sugar
200ml water
350ml vodka (unflavoured)
2 tbsp natural almond extract
2 tsp vanilla extract

1. Put the sugars in a saucepan with the water and slowly bring to the boil, stirring until the sugar has completely dissolved. Simmer for 1 minute, then turn off the heat and leave to cool.
2. Add the vodka and almond and vanilla extracts and stir well. Pour into a large jug.
3. Pour the amaretto through a funnel into a sterilized bottle and seal. Store in a cool dark place for up to a year.

Cook's notes

This amaretto is ready to serve straight away. The extracts may separate after several months but this isn't a problem; you just need to remember to give the bottle a quick shake before pouring.

Amaretto works well in both chocolate and fruit desserts. It has a particular affinity with apricots, peaches and cherries.

To make an 'amaretto sour' (a sour is a drink with a base liqueur, lemon or lime juice and a sweetener), put 5 tablespoons amaretto, 2 tablespoons fresh lemon juice and ½ teaspoon caster sugar into a cocktail shaker. Add a few ice cubes and shake well. Strain or pour into a glass, adding the classic decoration of a fresh orange slice and a maraschino cherry, if liked.

Amaretti Biscuits

Makes 30

Preheat the oven to 180°C/fan 170°C/gas 4. Line two baking sheets with baking parchment. Lightly whisk 1 egg white with a fork until slightly frothy. Add ¼ teaspoon almond essence and 2 teaspoons **amaretto** and whisk again. Put 175g ground almonds into a bowl and sift over 120g icing sugar. Make a hollow in the middle and add the egg-white mixture. Mix to a stiff dough. Divide the dough into 30 pieces and roll each into a ball. Place on the prepared baking sheets, spacing slightly apart, and flatten very slightly to stop them rolling off the sheets. Bake for 12 minutes or until dark golden-brown. Dust with icing sugar while still hot. Leave to cool on the baking sheets for 2–3 minutes, then transfer to a wire rack to cool completely. When cold, wrap in pairs in pastel-coloured tissue paper and store in an airtight tin.

Cherry Berry Cordial

Hopefully you made enough fresh fruit cordials to last you through the winter months. If not, this cordial can be made with frozen fruits, either from your freezer or try a mixed bag of 'summer fruit' from the supermarket.

Keeps for 2 months
Makes about 500ml

450g frozen mixed fruits such as cherries, raspberries, strawberries and
   redcurrants
350g caster sugar
2 tsp red wine vinegar
300ml water

1. Put the fruit (defrosted or still frozen), sugar and vinegar in a large saucepan. Add 4 tablespoons of the water, then heat gently, stirring occasionally, until the sugar has completely dissolved. Cook over a very low heat for 8–10 minutes until the mixture is a thick pulp.
2. Spoon into a fine-meshed plastic or stainless steel sieve and rub the purée through into a clean pan. Return the seeds and any pulp left in the sieve to the original pan. Add the remaining water and heat gently, then sieve again into the pan containing the fruit purée.
3. Bring the sieved mixture to the boil and simmer for 1 minute. Turn off the heat and leave to cool for 10 minutes.
4. Pour into small, warm, sterilized bottles and seal. The cordial will keep unopened for two months in a cool dark place. Once opened, store the cordial in the fridge, or freeze in small plastic bottles.

Cook's notes

Serve the cordial diluted to taste with sparkling water or soda water and ice.

Mixes of frozen fruit occasionally contain bananas; don't add these to this cordial as they will spoil the flavour and keeping qualities.

Christmas Chocolate Liqueur

This luxurious liqueur is perfect for after dinner and is probably best served after a light meal and simple fruit dessert, as it is very rich and creamy. It also makes a great gift when visiting friends.

Keeps for 1 month
Makes about 750ml

75g plain chocolate
150ml full-fat milk
½ x 397g can sweetened condensed milk
150ml double cream
1 tsp vanilla extract
200ml vodka (unflavoured)

1. Break the chocolate into squares and place in a heatproof bowl with the full-fat milk. Put the bowl over a pan of barely simmering water and leave for 5 minutes, then stir until the chocolate has melted and mixed into the milk.
2. Remove the bowl from the pan and whisk in the condensed milk. When completely blended, stir in the double cream and vanilla extract. Leave to cool.
3. Stir in the vodka, then chill in the fridge for 2–3 hours. Decant the chocolate liqueur into small sterilized bottles, seal and store in the fridge. Drink within one month of making.

Cook's notes

Use a good-quality dark chocolate with at least 85% cocoa solids for this liqueur, not a sweet plain chocolate, as the condensed milk will sweeten the mixture.

Don't use low-fat or 'light' versions of milk, condensed milk or cream when making this as they may cause the liqueur to separate.

This makes a very thick liqueur. Check the consistency after chilling and before bottling and stir in a little extra milk or vodka if you prefer a thinner result.

You can freeze the remaining condensed milk (decant into a small plastic container first) to use in baking or for another batch of liqueur.

Clementine and Cinnamon Cordial

This is a lovely Christmassy cordial and a great way of using up clementines if you've succumbed to too many 'buy one get one free' offers and your fruit bowl is overflowing!

Keeps for up to 2 weeks
Makes about 300ml

200ml water
100g caster sugar
1 stick cinnamon
8 clementines
1 lime

1. Put the water, sugar and cinnamon stick into a medium saucepan and slowly bring to the boil, stirring occasionally, until the sugar has dissolved. Reduce the heat and gently simmer for 5–6 minutes.
2. Meanwhile, halve the fruit and squeeze out all the juice. Strain the juice into the pan, bring back to the boil and simmer for a further 2 minutes.
3. Turn off the heat and leave to cool. Skim any froth off the top and remove the cinnamon stick.
4. Pour into sterilized bottles through a funnel and seal. Store in the fridge for up to two weeks, or freeze in small plastic bottles. Serve diluted.

Variations

You can use mandarin oranges instead of clementines. The lime adds a slight tanginess and brings out the flavour of the clementines. Use the juice of half a lemon, if you prefer.

Leave out the cinnamon for an unspiced version of this orange cordial.

Coffee Liqueur

Coffee-flavoured liqueur is a delight for both mixologists and cooks. Its popularity grew with the craze for the cocktail 'Black Russian', but it is also excellent in both coffee and chocolate desserts.

Keeps for up to 1 year
Makes about 1 litre

75g coffee beans
70cl bottle (700ml) white rum (Bacardi)
175g caster or granulated sugar
150ml water

1. Tip the coffee beans onto a chopping board and crack each one with the back of a metal spoon or the end of a rolling pin.
2. Put the coffee beans in a large, clean, sealable jar, such as a one-litre Kilner jar, and pour in the rum. Close the jar, give the mixture a gentle shake and leave in a cool dark place for five days.
3. Put the sugar and water in a saucepan and bring to the boil, stirring occasionally, until the sugar has completely dissolved. Bring to the boil and simmer for 2 minutes. Turn off the heat and leave to cool.
4. Add the syrup to the jar, stir to mix, then close and leave for a further two days.
5. Strain the coffee-infused rum into a jug, discarding the coffee beans. Pour into sterilized bottles. Seal and use within 12 months of making.

Variation

For coffee vodka, follow steps one and two, using unflavoured vodka instead of rum. Add 2 teaspoons caster sugar with the coffee beans in step 2. Leave out the sugar syrup (steps 3 and 4) and bottle as in step 5.

Tiramisu

Serves 6

This famous chilled coffee dessert is sometimes made with Marsala, but here coffee liqueur gives it a richer flavour. Put a 250g tub mascarpone in a bowl. Add 4 tablespoons golden caster sugar, then gradually stir in 600ml double cream. Add 5 tablespoons **coffee liqueur** and whisk until the mixture has the consistency of thickly whipped cream. Mix 2 tablespoons coffee granules with 300ml near-boiling water and leave until warm. Dip 175g sponge (boudoir) fingers into the warm coffee, a few at a time, until soaked but not soggy, and arrange a layer over the base of a shallow dish. Spread over half of the cream mixture. Grate 50g plain chocolate and sprinkle half over the top. Repeat with the remaining sponge fingers, coffee and cream mixture. Cover and chill for several hours or overnight (this dessert can be made up to 48 hours before serving). Sprinkle over the remaining grated chocolate and 1 teaspoon cocoa powder before serving.

Crème de Cacao

Commercial crème de cacao (chocolate liqueur) comes in two versions: a brown chocolate subtly flavoured with vanilla, and a clear 'white' version which is much sweeter. This home-made recipe replicates the former, rich and delicately sweet with a touch of bitter chocolate.

Keeps for 2 years
Makes about 750ml

70g cacao nibs (see Cook's notes)
350ml vodka
250g caster or granulated sugar
200ml water
2 tsp vanilla extract

1. Put the cacao nibs in a large, clean, sealable jar, such as a one-litre Kilner jar, and pour over the vodka. Close the jar and store in a cool, dark place for seven days, giving the jar a gentle shake every two days.
2. Put the sugar in a saucepan with the water and slowly bring to the boil, stirring occasionally, until the sugar has completely dissolved. Simmer for 2–3 minutes. Turn off the heat and allow to cool, then stir in the vanilla extract.
3. Add the syrup to the vodka mixture, stir well, then close and leave for a further day.
4. Strain the crème de cacao through a fine-meshed sieve or a muslin-lined colander and pour into a clean bottle. Seal and store in a cool dark place. Use within a year of making.

Cook's notes

Use a good-quality vanilla extract not essence for this liqueur, for the best flavour.

Cacao nibs are pieces of cacao (cocoa) beans; basically unsweetened chocolate before it's turned into chocolate. The cacao pods are harvested from trees which grow in tropical climates, mostly in South America. Choose cacao nibs according to the type of flavour you would like in your liqueur. They may be roasted, or left raw, and the pulp surrounding the beans left to ferment and drain, which reduces the beans' bitterness. They are available from some health food stores or may be purchased by mail order.

As well as a liqueur, crème de cacao can be used to boost the flavour of chocolate desserts.

Variations

The liqueur may be flavoured with almond extract instead of vanilla or with chilli or cinnamon for a spicy flavour: add a couple of dried red chillies or a stick of cinnamon with the cacao nibs.

You can also make this with a base of rum or whisky if you prefer.

Chocolate Torte

Serves 8

Put 100g chopped plain chocolate and 2 tablespoons **crème de cacao** in a small heatproof bowl set over a pan of steaming but not boiling water and leave until melted. Remove the bowl from the heat, stir and leave until cool. Preheat the oven to 170°C/fan 160°C/gas 3. Cream together 100g unsalted butter and 100g caster sugar in a large bowl until light and fluffy. Separate 3 medium eggs and beat the yolks into the creamed butter and sugar mixture, one at a time. Stir in the cooled chocolate, then fold in 50g crushed amaretti biscuits (page 121) and 60g sieved plain flour. Whisk the egg whites until stiff, then whisk in 1 tablespoon caster sugar. Fold into the chocolate mixture, a half quantity at a time. Turn the mixture into a loose-bottomed base-lined, buttered and floured 20cm tin, and bake for 30 minutes or until just firm to the touch. Leave to cool in the tin for 10 minutes, then remove and cool on a wire rack. Dust with icing sugar and serve slightly warm drizzled with **crème de cacao** and served with whipped cream.

Egg Nog

This isn't a cordial, syrup or liqueur, but an indulgent, creamy drink which should be served in small portions; there's enough here for six to eight. Enjoyed in both Scandinavia and America, this is a traditional Christmas drink.

Keeps for 2–3 days
Makes about 1 litre

300ml full fat milk
Strip of orange rind
1 cinnamon stick
4 medium eggs
100g caster sugar
½ tsp freshly grated nutmeg
300ml double cream
4 tbsp dark rum
100ml brandy

1. Pour the milk into a small pan, add the orange rind and cinnamon stick and gently heat until steaming hot. Turn off the heat, cover the pan with a lid and leave to infuse until cool. Remove the orange rind and cinnamon stick and chill the flavoured milk in the fridge.
2. Whisk the eggs until frothy, add the sugar and whisk again until thick and creamy. Whisk in about half of the nutmeg.
3. Whisk in the double cream, rum and brandy, adding each separately and gradually; the egg nog should be thick and creamy.
4. Chill in the fridge before serving in small chilled glasses, with a little of the remaining freshly grated nutmeg sprinkled on the top of each. Make up to a day ahead of serving and store in the fridge for no longer than 2–3 days.

Cook's note

Always use very fresh eggs from a reliable source when making egg nog. Raw eggs should not be used in food prepared for pregnant women or the elderly, or anyone whose health is compromised.

Variation

For a warm whisky version, whisk 4 egg whites (you can use pasteurized ones from a carton if preferred) with 1 tablespoon caster sugar until stiff peaks form when the whisk is lifted. In a separate bowl, whisk 4 egg yolks with 50g caster sugar until thick and creamy. Slowly whisk in 4 tablespoons whisky, 200ml full-fat milk and 100ml double cream. Transfer to a heavy-bottomed pan and cook over a very low heat, stirring with a wooden spoon, until the mixture has thickened slightly. Remove from the heat and fold in the whisked egg whites, half at a time. Ladle into warmed, heatproof glasses and grate a little nutmeg over each. Serve straight away.

Honeyed Apricot Liqueur

This sweet golden liqueur is a great addition to fruit salads or spooned over hot puddings with nuts or fruits such as apricots, peaches, plums or apples. Use Hunza apricots – although the wrinkled, brown-colour fruit is unattractive, it gives this liqueur a fantastic rich almondy flavour and golden colour.

Keeps for 1 year
Makes about 1 litre

300g Hunza apricots
700ml white wine
150ml clear honey
200ml brandy or rum

1. Rinse the apricots in a colander under cold water. Drain well, then tip into a large bowl. Pour over the wine, cover and leave to soak overnight.
2. Snip each apricot with kitchen scissors to reveal the stone (this helps flavour the liqueur). Put both apricots and wine in a large saucepan, add the honey and gently heat, stirring occasionally.
3. Bring the mixture to simmering point, but do not boil or the alcohol will evaporate. Keep just below simmering point for 2–3 minutes, then turn off the heat, cover the pan with a lid and leave to cool.
4. Return the apricots and wine mixture to the rinsed out bowl, cover and leave for 48 hours.
5. Strain the mixture through a sieve into a large jug. Stir in the brandy or rum, then pour into sterilized bottles. Seal and store in a cool dark place for at least one month before serving.

Cook's note

Use the soaked apricots in baking or desserts (remove the stones first) or in savoury dishes such as a lamb tagine. They can be frozen for up to two months.

Steamed Apricot Honey Pudding

Serves 6

Grease a 900ml pudding basin and line the base with a circle of baking parchment. Spoon in 1 tablespoon **honeyed apricot liqueur** mixed with 2 tablespoons honey and turn so that the mixture coats the bottom half of the basin. Put 150g fresh fine white breadcrumbs, 100g demerara sugar, 50g self-raising flour and 1 teaspoon baking powder in a bowl and stir together. Make a hollow in the middle. Add 25g softened butter, 1 medium egg beaten together with 2 tablespoons semi-skimmed milk and 200g chopped soaked apricots (left over from the honeyed apricot liqueur). Mix together to make a stiff batter. Spoon into the pudding basin, cover the top with pleated baking parchment and foil and tie with string. Use more string to make a handle. Put the basin in a heavy-based saucepan and pour in enough boiling water to come halfway up the side of the basin. Cover and steam for 1 hour 45 minutes, topping up with more boiling water if necessary. Carefully remove from the saucepan and remove the paper and foil covering. Loosen the sides of the pudding with a blunt knife, then place a serving plate on top of the basin and invert it. Shake gently to remove the pudding. Spoon over 4–5 tablespoons apricot liqueur before serving with hot custard.

Irish Cream Liqueur

This gloriously rich and creamy liqueur will rival any shop-bought cream liqueur and makes a fantastic gift to take to a dinner party. It only takes minutes to make and the quantities are easily divisible, so blend a smaller amount if you prefer.

Keeps for 3 weeks
Makes about 750ml

200g dulce de leche
2 tsp instant coffee
2 tsp near-boiling water
1 tsp vanilla extract
200ml brandy
300ml single cream

1. Spoon the dulce de leche into a large jug or bowl and stir to loosen. Blend the coffee and water together, then add to the dulce de leche with the vanilla and brandy. Stir well.
2. Add the cream and stir again until everything is blended together.
3. Pour into cold, sterilized bottles and seal. Store in the fridge for up to three weeks.

Cream Liqueur and Chocolate Cheesecake

Serves 6

Gently melt 50g butter in a saucepan. Stir in 100g crushed plain chocolate digestive biscuits. Spoon into the base of an 18cm loose-bottomed cake tin or spring-release tin and press down well with the back of the spoon. Chill for 30 minutes. Measure 600g full-fat cream cheese into a large bowl and beat until soft, then stir in 2 tablespoons **Irish cream liqueur**. Sift over 100g icing sugar, preferably unrefined, and stir in with 75g grated plain chocolate. Whip 300ml double cream until soft peaks form and fold into the mixture. Spoon into the tin on top of the biscuit base and smooth the top. Sprinkle over 25g grated plain chocolate. Leave in the fridge for several hours. Carefully loosen the sides of the biscuit crust with a small palette knife, then push up the base or remove the sides of the spring-release tin and slide the cheesecake onto a serving plate. Serve with extra Irish cream liqueur, if liked.

Krupnikas

This Lithuanian honey liqueur has a sweet and spicy fragrance and a gorgeous pale gold colour. It's ready to drink a few weeks after making, but the flavour mellows and matures with age; if you can, try to keep for six to twelve months before sampling.

Keeps for 2 years
Makes about 1.5 litres

1 vanilla pod
2 cardamom pods
1 cinnamon stick
2 whole cloves
2 whole allspice berries
¼ tsp freshly grated nutmeg
Large strip of lemon rind
200ml water
500g clear honey
70cl bottle (700ml) unflavoured vodka

1. Split the vanilla pod in half lengthways and put in a heavy-based saucepan. Remove the papery green skin from the cardamom pods and add the seeds to the pan. Add the cinnamon stick, cloves, allspice berries, nutmeg, lemon rind and water.
2. Slowly bring to the boil, lower the heat, cover with a lid and gently simmer for 5 minutes. Turn off the heat and leave the spices to infuse for 30 minutes.
3. Heat again until the mixture is steaming hot, then pour through a fine-meshed sieve or muslin-lined colander into a jug. Add the honey to the hot spicy liquid and stir well. Leave to cool.
4. Stir the vodka into the spicy honey mixture, then pour into sterilized bottles and seal. Store in a cool, dark place for up to 18 months. Serve cold or warm.

Cook's notes

There are many recipes for krupnikas, often passed from one generation to the next. Some contain spices such ginger, turmeric root (which gives a stunning gold colour to the liqueur), black peppercorns and orange rind. Adjust the spices when making this to suit your personal preference.

Served warm, this makes a soothing drink for a sore throat or cold.

Lemon Cordial

If you don't like the long list of additives in commercial lemon squash, try making this lemon cordial – it contains just three simple ingredients: sugar, lemons and water. Served diluted with cold water, it is the ultimate thirst-quencher and is also good with tonic water.

Keeps for up to 4 months
Makes about 1 litre

8 large unwaxed lemons
500g caster or granulated sugar
400ml water

1. Thinly pare the rind from four of the lemons, avoiding the white pith. Halve all the lemons and squeeze out the juice.
2. Put the lemon rind, juice and sugar in a saucepan and pour in the water. Gently heat, stirring occasionally, until the sugar has completely dissolved. Bring to boiling point, then turn off the heat.
3. Strain through a fine-meshed sieve into a jug, then decant immediately into hot sterilized bottles and seal.
4. Leave to cool, then store in the fridge for up to four months. To keep for up to a year, sterilize the bottles in a water bath (see page 10).

Variations

Lemon and lime cordial – use 3 large lemons and 6 large limes, using the finely pared rind of two of each fruit.

Orange cordial – use 6 large oranges and 1 large lemon, using the finely pared rind of 4 of the oranges.

Pink Lemonade – add 25g crushed raspberries when making the syrup.

Mulling Syrup

Nothing banishes the chills of winter like a warm glass of mulled wine. This spicy syrup can also be heated with a fruity cider or, for a non-alcoholic tipple, with apple, red grape or cranberry juice.

Keeps for 2 months
Makes about 450ml

For the mulling syrup
200g caster or granulated sugar
2 cinnamon sticks
5 whole cloves
5 allspice berries
1 tsp freshly grated nutmeg
5cm piece of fresh ginger, peeled and thinly sliced
Thinly pared rind of 1 unwaxed orange
750ml cold water
For the mulled wine
75cl bottle (700ml) medium fruity red wine
1 unwaxed orange, halved and thinly sliced

1. Put all the ingredients for the mulling syrup in a large saucepan and slowly bring to the boil, stirring occasionally until the sugar has dissolved.
2. Bring to a gentle boil and simmer uncovered for 15 minutes, until slightly reduced. Turn off the heat, cover with a lid and leave to cool.
3. Strain the syrup through a fine-meshed sieve or muslin-lined colander into a jug, then pour into a sterilized bottle. Store in the fridge for up to two months.
4. To make mulled wine, pour the red wine and syrup into a large pan. Add the sliced orange and gently heat until steaming hot, but do not boil. Ladle into warmed heatproof glasses.

Cook's notes

The syrup may be slightly cloudy rather than clear; this won't be noticeable when made into mulled wine.

When making mulled cider or mulled fruit juice, use half to two-thirds of the quantity of syrup initially, then taste and add a little more, depending on the sweetness of the cider or juice.

Clementine and Mulled Wine Jellies

Serves 4

Squeeze the juice from 300g (about 5) clementines into a jug and, if necessary, make up to 300ml with water. Add 6 sheets leaf gelatine and leave to soak for 5 minutes. Meanwhile, heat 300ml **mulled wine** until steaming hot and just below boiling point. Turn off the heat. Remove the gelatine leaves from the juice, add to the hot mulled wine and stir until completely dissolved. Stir in the juice and allow to cool. Pour into four wine glasses or serving dishes and chill for 3–4 hours until set. Serve topped with whipped cream, very lightly dusted with ground cinnamon or garnished with orange zest.

Orange and Lime Syrup

This syrup contains less sugar than most, which does mean it won't keep for long; once made, store it in the fridge. It's a great drink during the cold winter months as it gives a boost of vitamin C. The predominant flavour here is fresh orange with just a hint of lime to tame it.

Keeps for 3 weeks
Makes about 500ml

5 large unwaxed oranges
2 unwaxed limes
200ml water
75g caster sugar
1 tsp citric acid (see page 3)

1. Thinly pare the rind from 2 of the oranges, taking care to avoid the white pith, then pare one or two small strips from one of the limes. Put in a large pan with the water, sugar and citric acid.
2. Slowly bring to the boil, stirring occasionally, until the sugar has dissolved. Simmer for 2–3 minutes. Turn off the heat, cover the pan with a lid and leave to cool.
3. Meanwhile halve all the fruit and squeeze out the juice. Add to the pan and stir.
4. Strain through a sieve into a jug, discarding the orange and lime rind in the sieve. Pour into clean bottles and store in the fridge for up to three weeks. Dilute to taste.

Cook's notes

To extract more juice from the citrus fruit, put them one at a time in the microwave and heat for just a few seconds.

Although oranges are at their best and cheapest during the early months of the year, they are available all year round. During the hot summer months make this syrup to use in Spanish sangria: mix 3 parts red wine with 1 part orange and lime cordial, then dilute with 2 parts sparkling water, or to taste. Serve with ice, fresh mint and extra slices of oranges and lime, if liked.

Pomegranate Cordial

This bright red-coloured cordial makes a long, refreshing drink when served over ice topped up with sparkling water. It is also a good addition to dry fizzy wine on a special occasion. It's not quite as thick and syrupy as commercially produced grenadine, but it can be used in the same way.

Keeps for 3 weeks
Makes about 300ml

6 pomegranates
75g granulated sugar
1 tsp citric acid (see page 3)

1. Halve the pomegranates, then extract the juice by gently but firmly pressing each half over a lemon squeezer. Pour the juice through fine-meshed sieve into a saucepan.
2. Add the sugar and citric acid and slowly bring to the boil, stirring frequently until the sugar has completely dissolved.
3. Simmer for 1 minute, then turn off the heat and leave to cool. Pour into sterilized bottles. Store in the fridge for up to three weeks or freeze in small plastic bottles.

Cook's notes

Pomegranates are cultivated in South America, California, the Middle East and the Mediterranean. They are available all year round but the best season to buy in Britain is between September and December.

This fruity cordial makes good ices and sorbets and its acidity also makes it useful in marinades, especially for game, poultry and lamb.

Tequila Sunrise

Serves 1

This classic cocktail takes its name from the way the grenadine first sinks in the glass of tequila and orange juice and then rises to the surface. Add the **pomegranate cordial** quickly, pouring it down the back of a spoon so that it sinks to the bottom of the glass: Half-fill a tall glass with crushed ice. Pour in 2 measures/3 tablespoons tequila and 4 measures/6 tablespoons freshly squeezed orange juice. Quickly pour in ½ measure/2 teaspoons **pomegranate cordial**. Serve straight away.

Planter's Punch

Serves 1

This colonial drink originates from West Indian sugar plantations and should be made with freshly squeezed citrus fruit. Mix 2 tablespoons lime juice, 2 tablespoons orange juice, 4 tablespoons dark rum and 1 tablespoon **pomegranate cordial** together with a dash of angostura bitters. Pour into a tall glass with ice and top up with lemonade or soda water.

Spiced Rum

This is a lovely warming winter drink and should be served neat at room temperature without ice. It also goes well with mixers, especially fruit juices such as orange or pineapple, and makes a very good rum and coke.

Keeps for several years
Makes 700ml

70cl bottle (700ml) dark rum
½ cinnamon stick
1 vanilla pod, split in half lengthways
Thin strip of orange rind
6 whole cloves
4 allspice berries
4 black peppercorns

1. Remove a glassful of rum from the bottle (so that the remaining ingredients will fit) and keep in a small bottle or jar. Add all the flavourings and spices to the rum bottle.
2. Put the lid on the bottle and give it a gentle shake. Store in a cool dark place for two to four weeks, shaking the bottle every few days.
3. When the rum flavour is to your liking, strain the rum through a fine-meshed sieve or muslin-lined colander into a jug.
4. Pour the spiced rum back into the bottle (or into a presentation bottle if preferred, or if you can't get some of the spices out of the original bottle). Top up with the reserved glassful of rum and seal the bottle. The rum can be served straight away or left for the flavours to mature for a few months before drinking.

Cook's note
Adjust the spices according to your liking. Try adding a slice of ginger, nutmeg, star anise or a dried red chilli. You may need to cut or break some of the spices to get them to fit through the neck of the bottle.

Index

acetic acid 4
almond 116, 120–1, 131
  almond biscotti 21
amaretti biscuits 121
amaretto 21, 119, 120–1
  amaretto sour 121
apricot
  honeyed apricot liqueur 134–5
  steamed apricot honey pud 135
autumn fruit pudding 93

banana and medlar teabread 105
barley water 68–9
base spirits 4–5
beech leaf noyau 11, 13, 14–15
berries 8
  cheat's berry crème brûlée 71
  cherry berry cordial 119, 122–3
  see also specific berries
biscotti, almond 21
biscuits, amaretti 121
black Russian 129
blackberry
  blackberry hot toddy 91
  blackberry shrub 87, 88–9
  blackberry whisky 11, 90–1
  crème de mure 5, 87, 96–7
blackcurrant
  blackcurrant cordial 45, 46–7
  crème de cassis 54–5
Bloody Mary 74–5
Boodle's fool 39
bottles 6–10, 12
bramble cordial 87, 92–3
brandy 5
  beech leaf noyau 14–15
  cherry brandy 5, 52–3

crème de mure 96–7
egg nog 132–3
honeyed apricot liqueur 134–5
Irish cream liqueur 136–7
quince ratafia 116–17
redcurrant shrub 72–3

cakes
  fruit cake 51, 53
  lavender cupcakes 67
  scented geranium sponge 83
  sticky rose syrup cakes 77
champagne, elderflower 45, 56–7
Charlie Chaplin 115
cheesecake, Irish cream and chocolate 137
cherry
  cherry berry cordial 119, 122–3
  cherry bounce 50–1
  cherry brandy 5, 52–3
  cherry cranachan 51
  cherry schnapps 53
  cherryade 45, 48–9
chocolate
  chocolate and Irish cream cheesecake 137
  chocolate torte 131
  Christmas chocolate liqueur 124–5
  crème de cacao 23, 119, 130–1
cider, mulled 143
cinnamon 12, 17, 50, 52, 77, 102, 107, 116, 131–2, 138, 142, 148
  and clementine cordial 119, 126–7
  and damson syrup 87, 98–9
citric acid 3–4, 30, 38, 58, 88, 144, 146
clementine
  and cinnamon cordial 119, 126–7
  and mulled wine jellies 143
coffee 136–7